Black Butterfly Dust

Jean-Yves Vincent Ciccariello Solinga

Lyrical Prose

Leaning Rock Press
Gales Ferry, CT

Copyright © 2023 Jean-Yves Solinga

All rights reserved. No parts of this publication may be reproduced, stored in a database or retrieval system, or transmitted, in any form or by any means, without the prior permission of the author or publisher, except by a reviewer who may quote brief passages in a review.

Leaning Rock Press
Gales Ferry, CT 06335
leaningrockpress@gmail.com
www.leaningrockpress.com

978-0-9998744-2-4, Hardcover
978-0-9998744-5-5, Softcover
978-0-9998744-8-6, eBook

Library of Congress Control Number: 2023904233

Publisher's Cataloging-in-Publication
(Provided by Cassidy Cataloguing Services, Inc.)

Names:	Solinga, Jean-Yves, author.
Title:	Black butterfly dust / Jean-Yves Vincent Ciccariello Solinga.
Description:	Gales Ferry, CT : Leaning Rock Press, [2023]	"Lyrical Prose."	Includes bibliographical references.
Identifiers:	ISBN: 978-0-9998744-2-4 (hardcover)	978-0-9998744-5-5 (softcover)	978-0-9998744-8-6 (ebook)	LCCN: 2023904233
Subjects:	LCSH: Culture--Poetry.	Social interaction--Poetry.	Social isolation--Poetry.	Humanity-- Poetry.	Nihilism--Poetry.	France--Poetry.	LCGFT: Poetry.	BISAC: POETRY / General.
Classification:	LCC: PS3619.O4326 B53 2023	DDC: 811/.6--dc23

Printed in the United States of America

Dedication

I would like to dedicate *Black Butterfly Dust* to
my wife Elaine, for her support;
as well as my son Robert, his wife, Elizabeth and son Luc...
my daughter Nicole, her husband Marc and their daughters:
Noëlle and Luciana.

My vision into all of their futures is and has been
an endless source of optimism.

Jean-Yves Vincent Ciccarello Solinga
Gales Ferry, Connecticut, 2023

Acknowledgments

The specific pursuit of both, the well-written word and expressions of coherent ideas... which is the goal of this collection of lyrical prose, is a victory for the human spirit... in the age of artificial intelligence. It is therefore, to the enormous credit of individuals and publishers like Robin Nelson and Leaning Rock Press, for entrusting their name to my art and style of writing, a in world where often, a premium is given to fast and efficient communications... with streams of abbreviations and depleted sentence-constructions; as the fashionable norm.

Table of Contents

Preface 1
Black Butterfly Dust 9
Of Arthur Rimbaud and Jimi Hendrix 12
Exquisite Humanism 13
Fiction Encased Into Reality 15
Hauntingly Physical Presence 17
Humans... Discovering the Universe 19
Teenagers Into Adults 20
Like Orphans Playing in the Orphanage's Playground . . 21
Martian Chronicles Revisited 23
Miettes de souvenirs 24
Souvenir-Crumbs 25
The poet... Rereading his Poems. 26
A Greek Temple... As Its Foundation... 27
Glorious Return to Paris 35
A Virility in Her Voice 37
Wine in the Streets 39
Weapons into Plowshares 41
Weapons Designer 42
Lifeless Glance 43
Time Started... 44
Visiting Daddy at Work 45
Under the Skin 46
Unrepentant Humanist in the Entrails of an M.R.I. 48
To that Unknown Soldier... 50

Kafka... Revisited.	52
Jamestown Revisited.	53
Just Some Syllables	55
Returning From the Atrocities of War.	56
Noilly Prat	57
A Nihilist's Fervent Wish.	58
A Place That Only Exists in Poetry	59
A Lyrical Incursion into Her Sexuality	60
A Mother's Tomato-Dressing	62
Neanderthal Man in Charge	63
Of Kisses Under the Bridges of the Seine	65
Tickets Only	67
Musical Odyssey	68
The Voices of Angels	69
The Simplicity of Happiness	71
The Shape of Clouds.	72
A Cold Winter-Night.	73
Artists Swallowed by Their Universe	75
The Death of Some Trees.	77
A Last Sumptuous Meal.	78
A pre-Deified Universe	79
Magical Sandwich.	81
A Virility in Her Voice.	82
All the While.	84
And Humans "Constructed" the Universe	85
Artificial Dreams	86
Between "Boogie Wonderland" and Reality	88
Between Kabul and Kashmir.	89
"Black-Folk" Cemetery	91
"Congolese Hell".	92
Like Poetry on Silk	93
Cultivating Our Gardens	95
Ode to the "Septic-Pumping" Business	97
Death in Paris	98
Death in the Barnyard	102
Reincarnation	103
French Version of « Réincarnation »	105

Duality of This Woman 107
Monica 108
Dusty Kiss 110
Armstrong's Leap 111
Green-Eyed World 112
Deconstruction of "Babar the Elephant" 113
Early Fall in Saint Émilion 115
In an Open Field of New England 116
Half-Slumber 117
Back to Cosmic Dust 118
El Maghreb 119
French Version of «El Maghreb» 120
And Humans "Constructed" the Universe 121
Epiphany of a Nihilist 122
In Defense of Real Human Tears 124
Church Festival 126
Religious Sharp Shooter 127
Les funérailles d'un père 129
A Father's Funerals 131
The Temerity of Innocence 133
For a Post-Paradisiac, Digital World 134
Lo Spasimo Della Vergine 135
Of Proustian Madeleines and Camembert 136
Wisps of Her 137
Jean-Yves Solinga, Poet 139
Other Books by Jean-Yves Solinga 144

Preface

Late 1950s. for them, typical wet-early Spring, in New England.

Father, mother, and son... new transplants from the "Garden of Year-long, blood-red, Canac flowers" of North Africa.

Not an auspicious beginning, for another day in the New World and twelve-hour workdays, in entry-level employment.

But... all new things, must have a start: the father had stopped the car, in an area still inhabited by active farm-tracts of descendants from the earliest European immigrant-settlers.

But these newer Catholics... Franco-Italian family had not always been welcomed as newcomers into the reputed territory of Protestant-ethics and postcard-birth of the Thanksgivings of history books.

It could, therefore, feel very lonely, for non-English speakers, in these, pre-internet, pre-everything days.

So... a drive, to kill time, through some wet, back roads: they came back with a foot-long, skinny... branch-like, off-spring, from a local tree (wrapped in cloth, like a foundling).

Decades later. The father and mother long dead. And the son, having found his professional legs in his American life, had decided to come back to that neighborhood. That backyard... where the father had dug and "installed" that twig. He could still see him kneeling on the cold wet goo... assiduously scraping with his bare fingers, to make a cradle for the plant. And now, inside the comfort of a car, he couldn't even recognize the house, his bedroom window... the back of the yard!

A majestic... green force of nature, stood in the very spot where his father's fingers had been. The son... now... a writer... a lyrical writer... a nihilist obsessed by ethics: in his world... with no apparent divine guidance: whose very pivotal friendship was from a "wandering defrocked. priest"... so this majestic tree, seems as good an anchor, as any, for a preface.

The son did not need much encouragement to extrapolate [a new term he had just learned in his college prep Algebra class] ... that he had been protected by a family cocoon from the low-income realities on the other side of the flimsy, paper-thin front door.

Not yet, fully taking the measure of the insulating power of the splendid mother's meals, around a wobbly converted card table.

Or being reminded of it, when asked by one of his less-savory teenage neighbors, "You drink wine and beer with your father! Can you get us a couple of cans?"

Having been cajoled in the quasi-aristocratic professions of his parents' status as upper bureaucrats in the old world, he very quickly realized that school and academic degrees would be his keys to further survival and maybe any hope of success: at least physical!

It turned out that both, the twig and the son, did well.

So, in a way, this preface is more a combination of an ode to the New World... critical analysis... and report card of his [of my ?] ingredients for the Genesis of this book

---

The value of Michel Eyquem, Sieur de Montaigne's love for a style - a mode of writing- l'essai... [the Essay}... has always been attractive to me.

From the French verb "essayer"… to "attempt". It is one of the reasons, why I had been warned by a dissertation advisor: "Jean-Yves… this is beautifully written… flowing in both languages… but it is supposed to be research… not poetry!"

Montaigne purposefully retreated to one of the Medieval towers of his cattle [in one of the best regions in France for pâté!]. He'd had a successful social and political career; but left active interactions, in order to write and in the process, popularized, the essay-genre as a perfect tool for further analysis of "la nature humaine": wanting to delve into its universal traits (if any).

The necessary isolation, imposed by the pandemic during a good part of this book, presented me with an apparent similar situation [maybe, even the same contradictions]: i.e. Montaigne having, on one hand, locked himself away from society to ironically study human behavior… to better understand… the human mind… in its social settings!

And it is hopefully, indeed how I have approached the topics dealing with some of my larger interests. That is, mining information about our apparently irreconcilable leftovers of our evolution from… beasts… to more intelligent beasts! But beasts with the sort of brains… that can reflect on their own actions. Thus, able to attach value-judgment on acts and thoughts. Amazing evolution on our part! For… if the remaining primates can be almost as smart [even cunning] as we are, they have yet, to form… to write… sacred… and legalistic texts and even kill over value-judgements !!!. … the color of a flag… or one's views, of an immaculate conception, during the European religious wars.

What is it, therefore, that we can …not deduce, but induce [i.e. from the particular to the general]? From the One… to the Many? What can we learn from one person? From our very self? And even produce books of lyrical prose in the process?

Montaigne loosely answered the question… with a question. Shyly asking: "que sais-je"? … what do I know? … not even, daring a negative affirmative answer: "I do not know"!

And thus, after losing my favorite table and assorted members of an [at times] unusual assortment for a human comedy troop of actors, at Bartleby's coffee house in Mystic… I moved to my dining room… the spot from which I have… and still raise, my first glass of wine with family.

Talking about feasts! What about the "Movable Feast" that is Paris? The immediate need to want to absorb the beauty of Paris has often highlighted its duality to me.

Such human conditions as "life and living"… but with their nagging opposites: Loneliness and Despair!

Victor Hugo's Paris, for instance, is a study in contrasts [the beautiful Esmeralda and the ugliness of Quasimodo!]. The Paris of Yves Montand [the feminine identity of the city and the masculine identity of the thunder]… versus Gilbert Bécaud [and his dates] versus Charles Trénet [with the innocence of a school boy] versus Charles Aznavour [and the Bohemian life of the city]. And, of course, the tortured Charles Baudelaire… [a tender soul… attracted hopelessly by the evil of the streets]!!

All of these people and places invaded during my expatriate years during the chaotic 60s and 70s: From "Clair-Obscur of the Soul"… to "Rage and Passion".

In these former collections and continuing with this one… I write about that universal thing, in each of us, that tries to make sense [for instance] of today's Paris lovers and their feeling… that jealous specters of past lovers, still haunt the city… in such poems as "Death in Paris"… "Glorious Return to Paris"… "To live and die in Paris"… and so many more!

Montaigne must have suspected that we had a common source for those common human traits, well before DNA.

Nuggets of the universal, in each of us, were suspected by writers and artists….that from a basic, similar building-blocks origin of our make-up, the individual… contained the universal in [their] make-up.

Montaigne, artists, playwrights… street-accordion players, must have suspected a replicating framework that linked…all of us… to all of us.

Thus, the ease of linking lyrically, such different individuals, as Juliette Gréco, Jimi Hendrix, and Arthur Rimbaud.

And of course, only Paris could have been responsible for the way Gréco and Miles Davis fell in love!

At any rate, here I was… at my desk, supervising my yard… all alone for months, writing about women… men… as social animals!

Reconstructing [or inventing], torrid moments… overlooking a New England blizzard! And… having learned something from the thousand pages of "Doctor Zhivago"… the bedroom eyes of Omar Sharif… sumptuous lips of Julie Christie… and voice-over, reciting the lyrical mood of the good doctor: a few feet away from the fur-covered nakedness of Christie!

That! … to this writer… is my answer to human dominance over machines! Algorithms have yet to self-start… due to the infection of jealousy in the coding!

He had learned to neatly pack his immigrant tools and divide his world in insulated, separate pockets: i.e. the duality of the sources of the title in English and French of his first book of poetry: "Clair-Obscur of the Soul".

Worlds of litanies! Wealth of contrasts! In which, the author: first or third person, manipulates the universe at will.

"Black Butterfly Dust" continues that process.

He [the son] very quickly learned to appreciate and take the full measure of his own cultural nuanced, pro-European… pro-French biases and not directly attack, in geo-political discussions of pre-Foreign Service, undergraduate studies. Not instigate, with some awkward adjective, and not fall, in the give-and-take, to the cultural ad hominem attacks.

He envied how a fellow classmate and close friend [of British origin], seemed immune to this risk.

Such mindless generalizations found in his early university, political sciences class as… " Charles de Gaulle is a communist!… "He…[the general] does not like us… unlike England that does!" Telescoping five hundred years of Franco-British fighting [in a nutshell of Churchill/Roosevelt vs de Gaulle] and not taking into account how historically [for instance] the French Revolution [and the only other Republic] had become the biggest threat to the British and other monarchies everywhere!

I have scrupulously, from my first published poem "Iced Grass and Lost Youth", highly fictionalized the first person singular or blended any suspiciously identical, main character avatar, in the text.

But I cherish the flexibility of an overarching dreamscape… because it feeds, energizes, and grounds my writing. Having seen, eaten, smelled, kissed… foreign and extremes things from my youth.

Sidi Moussa and Paris are state of mind settings… my writings are not travelogs. Hence my poems recognize the kinship with Led Zeppelin's "Kashmir" and the landscape of my "El Maghreb".

But some necessary, historic details have to be wrapped in the time-honored way of the Fables or Religious texts, full of ornamental imagery. Parabolas with double or triple meanings!

So is it, with this couscous royal of my youth.

Meals are particularly suited for those multiple interpretations and outcomes! [i.e., the last supper]

This highly fictionalized Couscous Royal is a compilation of evenings which endangered the lives of the persons involved!

The issue was the brotherly friendship between two men who could not give any hints of it without putting their families at risk.

It was at the beginning of the end of the French Protectorate in the Maghreb and the quasi-surrealistic need to ignore emotions: men… highly respected leaders… established in their respective camps. Speaking each other's language. Knowing each other's culture. Both with a visceral, natural attraction to the North African dirt and getting their strength from it… like the Titans of old from their Mother-Earth!

Thus came the time of adieux, of the last couscous… which had all the trapping of Greek tragedies. Two enemies… crying in each other's embrace! The mutual courage and unadulterated symbols. They would become the "Other" to each other in the morning!

The "Reality encased in Fiction" of this collection… is made of deadly ball-bearings in a slingshot and not the aromatic dates from the enormous trees outside the movie house, where I was introduced to James Dean!

The sort of dilemma, that can also occur quietly, in some of my poems, in the nuptial ambiance of a Parisian bedroom.

And yet, other passages' tipping points in my work, have other complexities. Like a son's love for his dying father and the astonishing humanity of a young Captain, with articles of desertion in his hands and the biblical aura of King Solomon.

My poems have of course no practical answer(s)… anymore than, Romeo and Juliet… is a practical guide for a future High School guidance teacher… to instruct love-sick students.

The following book has the audacity to deal with those and other issues: avoiding absolutes. Having none to offer.

Not unlike Moses coming down the hill… but with Commandments in erasable ink.

Jean-Yves Vincent Solinga
Gales Ferry CT.
2023

Jean-Yves Vincent Ciccariello Solinga

Black Butterfly Dust

Near the ochre-tones of Tipasa's landscape, North Africa.

Infected by the most toxic element... that can be...
the *rage* of an adolescent fever:
when a youthful soul, still drives the flesh!

The senses, as sharp as ever.
Everything and anything...
reconstructing themselves... by themselves.

Some sort of invasive Faustian flow, of regenerative, sinful energy,
seemingly emanating from the passage of a wayward *butterfly*.

Time... that rare commodity.
Time... nemesis of moments of happiness.
And yet... maker of diamonds.

The glorious remaking of the past... down to its smallest, pulsating,
organic particle...
At the overlap of Baudelaire and Van Gogh,
where exists still, the miracle of a glorious *synesthesia*:

Such as, the purple of alcoholic-smells, from lavender fields,
filtered through semi-closed glances:
over taut, pink abdominal muscles.

Sensuality of acrid sweat,
upon collapsing from rushing down Montmartre to rue Saint Lazare.
The approving smile of *madame la concierge de l'hôtel*.
And the welcomed, miniscule dimension of the elevator cage.

Reconstruction of the past, from drops of romantic rain,
into puddles of magical dust... and Paris at our feet!

Powdery concentration of hallucinatory happiness:
Beyond the bounds of existential ethics.
But not beyond the culpability from ethics.

After all this time.
All these attempts at capturing time.

Trying to petrify sacred temple-fumes,
floating around statues on sun-scorched Mediterranean islands,
by inserting them into blue-veined Italian marble.

Or... burned on the artist's retina, by visions
of sanguine, glistening...
... fleshy folds, on museum walls.

The lyrical coloring of Monet
and carnality of Courbet.

A banquet for the palette, serving the extremes of appetites.
The viewer, seeing... with cool, feigned scholarship
his most intimate tastes... displayed for all to see!

Teenage echoes of whispered, plaintiff sighs:
echoing wistfully over hot Maghreban mirages.

Imposition of frozen, New *Englandish*, snow-covered roads,
On the adulthood routine of teaching.

Uncontrollable, reconstruction of frissons,
from absent touches on the forearm:
in the unpretentious, natural hedonism of Parisian promiscuity.
Cherished Proustian, Madeleine-hosts.
Aftertaste of sweet-treats, from these unseen presences.

Remaining humidity on lips.
Deep earthly things and people... more real than realities:
Simply through deep body-throbbing.

Wise forewarnings, from our cosmological starburst-birth past.
Reminders of our duality...
... of our primordial-mud ancestry
and yet...
our quasi-miraculous sentient capacities...
... to *know*.

Our Mythologies... invented... in order to distract
from a nagging sensation of our orphaned status.

Mythologies, invading such cold realism,
as Flaubert,
living in his romanticized world, with Madame Bovary.

Or the quasi-pubescent hopelessness of a Meursault,
imbibing the passing, perfumed-warmth
of the bikini-clad Marie.

To the glorious moments of humanity's own consciousness.

Of Arthur Rimbaud and Jimi Hendrix

Reality invades them…
they are "possessed" by the world…

Their "Realities"
enter them, through the capitulation of their body and mind.

The nuptials of all… and any true artist:
to themselves and their art.

An asexual act…
of complete submission to
that *OTHER*…

… that half-drunk, at the bar:
hearing…
Little Wing, in public… for the first time!!
Or
Rimbaud's first, declamation of the seminal "*Bateau Ivre*":
in a candle-lit soirée.

———

No artifice… no posing.
Practically, no audience.

The artist.
The truly, sacrificial lamb
-of human redemption and price-
for the privilege of artistic, human *creation*.

One of the closest acts of humanity's claim
to any divine genesis!

This… the honor of the artist's time on this earth:
-Rimbaud… Hendrix-
Sacrificed, on the altar of creativity.

Reflections on the tragic lives of some favorite artists.

Exquisite Humanism

He had heard about these blinding stars of academia...
The brightest among the brightest.

Impeccable trajectories of their firmament:
Degreed from the uber-best.
And they knew it!

Thick office oak-door.
An oppressively small floor space:
Seemingly, making the wrapping bookshelves look aggressive.

In new graduate student's spinning mind.
... Thinking to himself:
"It seems to lack only the fumes of temple incense".

The rest is, what must have first defined *humanism*,
in the mind of young scholars...

... as they sat in soft cotton, in the shade of white Greek temples.

A gentle, incredible, *approachable* intelligence:
A worldwide-recognized authority in his field!

The student's proposal for class presentation.
The tittle scribbled in pencil.

And then, these words of tranquility.
A quasi-biblical assuredness:
"Excellent topic... you'll see!"

Jean-Yves Vincent Ciccariello Solinga

Not a hint of arrogance or impatience...
Rather... a simple...
almost fatherly parting clarification...

... of what turned out to be his ...so-discrete...
directed correction!

Embellished, experienced personal moments, of genuine, exquisite humanism, in academic interaction, facilitating the transfer of knowledge. Prompted by a tête à tête with a world class renowned professor and anxious, first year graduate student.

Fiction Encased Into Reality

He could not remember… ever…
not loving…
and yet, not fearing… all around his house…
the *bled* of his youth.

It contained unpassable, repelling zones
of luxuriant high winter-grass.

Viper-infested, brittle summer-blades.

The always, cool gusts from the green Atlantic:
running over the hot, stillness of inner-land villages.

Hardened, mud-covered houses
that had seemingly sprouted from the surrounding dust.

———

He had been raised seamlessly between
the venerable *Baguette* and sacred *Kesra* bread.

Between *Maman-Barka* ** *and Maman-Maman.*

———

Nevertheless, as in the films noirs of the 30's:
the idealist protagonist is killed.***

The one…ironically… symbolically
so enamored…
with the illicit candied fruits: sold at side entrance of his Lycée.

The hopeless romantic
... eventually killed...
in a local, indigenous attack.

By deluded teenagers... with slingshots:
ironically, attacking a fervent supporter of their cause!

His last moments of life...
filled by visions and sadness of an idealized secular world:

A primitive... primordial... virginal space
-simply... and still-
and especially untouched
by religions.

** Barka: childhood caretaker, indigenous, Berber woman.
*** From a metal-ball bearing propelled by a slingshot.

His PhD. Dissertation on the Maghreb: an intellectual exercise, where deference is given to the precision of analysis rather than the exuberance of the heart. A world, for him, of necessary self-restraint. A voyage through the perfumed lyrical fauna of his youth... taking assiduous care to show evenhanded tonality due to the geo-political and colonial ramifications.

From "Notes on personal mythologies"... "Writing about the Maghreb, was like two lovers, of the 'Faustian charms' of the same woman, comparing their respective, lyrical notes about the source of their passion... he had to defend his love... not for his... but for the Other's landscape.

Loosely inspired by tragic, real events about an individual's assault. The price paid for their historical ideals and their overlap over realities: presented in the manner of "The "Singing Detective" [A Tormented and bedridden man and his debilitating disease. A mystery writer who relives his detective stories through his imagination and hallucinations].

Hauntingly Physical Presence

Remembering and listening to one of the last piano recitals, at the Memorial of virtuoso friend: "It felt like 19th century séance ... he was in the room!"

From his répertoire...
and the depth of his own typical youthfulness.

From all the musical treasures:
All the various encapsulations of the feathery world of children.

A berceuse! **
On that New England night!
A defying arrogance from the warmth of a cradle!

Early Fall, damp darkness:

His overlapping gift of supple keyboard dexterity,
Making one,
the intricate demands of the scored-irregularity of touch from his slender fingers.

Translating the strings of black notes from the cellulose:
Beyond verbalized lyricism.

―――――

And...
this very intimate apotheosis!
The *audio play-back* ** of that night!

Jean-Yves Vincent Ciccariello Solinga

Hearing, feeling....
the hauntingly *PHYSICAL* presence of his being:
such details as,
the background creaks from his body movements,
on a venerable century-old piano bench.

The tired squeak of the pedal-action,
against his elegant concert-shoes.

The whole night,
now being *re-played* by squiggles, of musical wave-lengths,
on the oscilloscope.

Seemingly transcribing my own heartbeats,
on my computer screen!

Transubstantiation
of the wood and metal of the piano!

The warmth of flesh and limpidity of blood!

Concluding with a sublime cascade from the upper register.
-Quasi-minerality of crystalline notes-

From the extreme right-side of keyboard.
Rain of musical shooting stars!

The cadence... like the child....
finally settling... into the warmth of a wooly eternity.

Nota bene. The poem is from extracts from "Notes of Personal Mythologies".
** Gottschalk's "Berceuse".
** My deep appreciation to Reenat Pinchas and Pam Ryley for the recording of this Berceuse played by Aymeric Dupré La Tour.

The poem is a very personal, visceral, reaction upon re-listening to what would turn out to be the author's last encounter with Aymeric.

Humans… Discovering the Universe.

Humans… discovering the universe,
thought that they had a hand in its design.

And in it,
the pieces of a pre-existing
-all-encompassing… swirling of left-overs-
primordial junk!

Humans… having made a home
-in the manner of prehistoric families-
in *prefab* Dordogne grottos.

On this planet:
A random, third rock, from a minor star.

———

And then,
humanity's marvelous *tour de force*:
taking ownership of things!

-Human's adapted and adaptive explanation-
Nomenclature.

———

Newtonian… Einsteinian formulae:
neatly tying these quasi, divine forces
on dusty, black boards.

Humanity's very own elegant answer to biblical creation:
Higher Mathematics.

Electrons… for a long while
had been unproductively circling around nuclei,
until humanity used them for light bulbs.

Comment by a slightly jaded, Ph.D. researcher, on a Krisper-like project: "Origin… what origin? It is not miraculous… it is simply there… it was always there… we simply discovered this thing!"

Jean-Yves Vincent Ciccariello Solinga

Teenagers Into Adults

Question in final, philosophy-exam: "Moments that define... in particular... the medical universe.

Former high school teacher:
reading newspaper by-line,
about a particular student's achievement.

A typical teenager:
An unlikely *existentialist activist*!

His lasting classroom presence, of Monday-mornings:
Sleep-deprived, glassy glances.

Typical immaturity of goals:
"End-of-day embrace with girlfriend".

Both of them fully attached
to the latest electronic wonder.

———

Ever-present agitation,
in this large teenager:
with large leg-muscle- twitch...waiting for any passing prey!

... and then, the news!
His professional, lifesaving action:

"The kid"... had managed
to DO...
-what many of us seldom get to do-
To embody...
what could have... would have simply remained...
-a teacher's lesson plan for the day-
... an embryonic entry...goal-entry... on a syllabus:
Subject: "What is *Commitment*?".

Comment by a Philosophy Professor, of his appreciation of the steadfast professionalism, as an attending medical staff, of one his former student, during his wife's labor at the regional hospital.

Like Orphans Playing in the Orphanage's Playground
A cosmological end-game fable

In some future time: Sentient life… still looking for a sense in its genesis.

The routine had become routine:
A cosmonaut had been assigned to explore a potentially rich sector.

Preparing his sensor,
the latter had a thought for one of his earthling ancestors:
Having just re-read, that earth-bound, excavations
had depleted most of the usable minerals on Earth.
And now…
following in the steps of his nineteenth century Alsatian coal-workers
family,
He was…in his turn…
exploring for the riches of a planet.

Standing with a space-age, analyzing prod:

Deep in a Martian cave:
"Ready to explore," he radioed!

―――――

The next sight, took his breath away:

Abandoned,
protected from deadly cosmic rays
and …
thousands of meters down into the Martian surface:
now, *deserted cities*!!

…
*Mars and its life… had evolved
and had either disappeared or left*

Jean-Yves Vincent Ciccariello Solinga

…Its inhabitants …
either dead or turned into parentless, space-wanderers:
And all this, while, when on Earth,
life…
had probably stared to exists as single-cell bacteria.
-Swimming in primordial soup-

Yes!… us…
-The eventual humans-
-The future conquerors of space!-

———

The cosmonauts… now, suspecting
that they were looking at a probable lonely future.

———

Taking a break from a game of tag,
one of the orphans tearfully says to his playmates:

"I have always fantasized that my parents would show up at the gates."

[From an unattributed movie scene]

Martian Chronicles Revisited

In the deep... deep future of humanity's fate.

The space capsule door had opened:
An endless greyish mineral-world, at his feet.

There were worlds out there:
Dead flying rocks!
... but this one, had given evidence of hopeful possibilities.

He looked down at his boots...
... he could not hold back his tears, on his still-helmeted face.

He could distinguish some sort of insect crawling:
Life!
With a brain, the size of a punctuation-comma!!
Some sort of beast!
The type he would nonchalantly find in his garden!

Looking up into the darkness of space,
He shamefully realized:

With all the technologies!
All the smart instruments!

... feeling some **kinship**
in the quaint febrility of this diminutive... deluded...
quasi-insect!

Miettes de souvenirs

Réflexions sur Paris

De retour… de son Odyssée,
et de ses rites de passage :
Présent… Passé… Présent.

Il ressentait une ambivalente satisfaction :
Imposant son propre univers
au milieu du lyrisme éternel parisien.

Le sien, malheureusement hanté
par l'inévitabilité… la certitude… de peines futures…
… au milieu-même de ces témoins architecturaux de ses bonheurs de jeunesse.

———

Il ne lui restera, alors
que l'orgueil de sa pensée humaine :
Face au silence éternel des choses.

Dans cette solidarité, avec les autres poètes et artistes,
qu'il croit bien avoir reconnus
aux pieds des pierres des tours de Notre Dame.

———

Ce parvis privilégié, depuis toujours, étant signe des multi-coexistences
de l'art créateur… du noir nihiliste…
et de l'âme poétique.

Souvenir-Crumbs

Reflections on Paris

Back from his Odyssey.
And its rites of passage:
Present… Past… Present.

He felt an ambivalent satisfaction.
Imposing its own universe
… in the very midst of eternal Parisian lyricism.

His… unfortunately haunted
by the inevitability … the Certainty… of future sorrows
… in the very midst of these witnesses
Of the joys of youth.

He will then, be left with only
the pride of human thought:
in the face of the eternal silence of Things.

In the solidarity
with other poets and artists,
whom he believes having recognized
at the foot of the stones of the towers of Notre Dame

The Parvis, being always the rich coexistence
of Creative art and black nihilism
of the poetic soul.

Jean-Yves Vincent Ciccariello Solinga

The poet… Rereading his Poems.

It was the entirety of HER glance upon him.
It had been there all the time!

Our very own reciprocal genesis:
Our creations…. recreating the artist in their own image!

May the gentle photons of sweetness illuminate this part of the cosmos!
Not unlike
what scientists say about the genesis of the universe:
*where we see things, so far away, that apparently still appear in our universe
well after their dissolution.*

It was hard to comprehend:
Everything that would become anything and everything
was there… in its infancy… at its beginning.

-In miniscule insignificant volume… but everything!!!-

Never made sense!... until… until, when he realized that…
All these moments… all the sighs…
All the whispers had been there!

His very presence… his very senses, gave them
a *human meaning*.
All… and yet regained… in the inert solidity of things.

All connected by this precious silk thread:
Human memory!
The artist… reliving through his art.

Reciprocal waves… one in front of each other
Giving substance to the other.

SHE… now… living…among everything!

A Greek Temple... As Its Foundation...

A romanticized, family biopic

By way of... and out of... the Maghreban and the province of Telagh, a French expatriate to America, comes back to his roots, decades later: to the city of Marseille. He is on the jetty of the famous fishing harbor, where his parents (world war one and world war two traumatized souls, played at the fountain of the nearby "panier" **[a maze of buildings, used by the French underground Maquis, and later, mostly dynamited by the Nazis].

He was back where it had started:
The entrance, to the "Vieux Port" of Marseille...
And the multiplicity of its exotic roots:

At the foot of the Romanesque église Saint Laurent
-with remains of a... real... *bone fide*... Greek temple in its basement:

Which painting, by Oncle Jules Ciccariello, hangs inspiringly
right behind the writer!

Civilizations upon civilizations!

A sociological "bouillabaisse" of rich local ingredients.
Akin, to its contradictory pungent, garlic-base and saffron perfume:
"His very own provençales Madeleines".

Sleepy nuptials
-in the semi-tropical heat-
... of concentrated, fermented fish-smells: from now, half-sleepy stalls.

Wake-up call, from the solar-solidity of the universe!
Return to reality:
caused by the incrusted, diamond-sharpness
of the granite into his upper thighs.

———

Looking to his left
-a whitish pebble in the ink-blue Mediterranean-
The fortress-*prison* of the Château d'If.
And to the right
-delineated unto the Provençal blue-
Notre Dame de la Garde.

Romanesque adventures:
The man in the iron mask.
And le Comte de Monte Christo:

Perfect personas…
Because realistic in fiction
and romantically believable in reality.

---

*The ideal midway point
In the author's artistic goals!*

The Realpolitik… of created worlds:
of hand-to-hand combat,
at the foot of the *Bonne Mère basilica*.

-Instead of destructive allies' *bombardements*-

…

Not resorting to destructive allies, carpet-bombing:
Using, instead, North-African troops,
to flush out the occupying Germans.

Magical city.
Visceral caldron of primordial human…
and documented human excesses.

Alexandre Dumas (père et fils) of romanesque… pseudo-real tales of…
Jealousies. Revenge. And pure evils.

Le Comte de Monte-Cristo.
L'homme au masque de fer.

But also... the classic simplicity of clueless love:
Marius and Fanny:
First filmed on the dock of my toddler-*father* playground.
The panoply of human emotions:
Worthy of any in the Classics of Greece…

Who happen to have founded Marseille!!

The intensity, of unadulterated, youthful lust.
Marius. Fanny. Cesar.
The survival of human values, over their stupidities and short comings.

All these pages and people, from *his* favorite novels:
"Alexandre Dumas and Marcel Pagnol"!
He sighed:
"If only, I could also bring such *things* into believable realities!"

———

He had come back to this city... on this stone jetty:
Like "le Penseur" by Pierre Rodin.

And also like a Titan... back to mother-earth.
To the *parental* feel of the streets.

Intoxicating synesthesia, from the iodized smells.
Out-of-body experience!

Ah!... yes... indeed! If only, we could take IT with us!

———

First rites-of-passage:
Full of awkward trepidations of unverbalized love.

That slight hesitation of his fingers
on her birdlike shoulders.

Semi-pre-verbal... pregnant glances:
Lingering at the end of their unfinished sentences.

The ease of conversation
-common to all first-time lovers-
without social artifice.

Jean-Yves Vincent Ciccariello Solinga

Unexplainable... visceral... organic... natural understanding
Of one... where there used to be...
... TWO!

———

Perfect setting of overlapping perspectives.
Multiple re-geneses of cherished moments...
... now...
... through the sorcery of lyricism!

Things and souls.
Souls and things.
The miracle of inverted fertilization of... his soul...
by the very *virility of her flesh.*

———

Grand-child of poor Neapolitan, fishermen.
Nineteenth century, cholera-dislodged families.

Now... here he is:
An avowed non-communicant of any... and all divinities:
Of any color or stripes!

A complicated double-nihilist!
Ironically orphaned... and yet,
a prodigal son, nevertheless.

With no identifiable beginning:
Except, for a given-name. to a given baby...
... *Solitary...* in Italian.

No satisfactory
Happy Hollywood ending.

———

Reverse, returning-refugee
from the so-called "new-world".

West to East, this time.
America! And its shallow-rooted and wasteful plasticity:
Proven in his eyes, since his first taste: in *Rebel without a cause.*

The destruction, by teen agers, of huge cars,
the size of his living room!

Now... on these stones:
Feeling the dying breaths of the African Sirocco.
The seemingly still warm,
friendly atoms, from his Maghreban youth:
Finding him, at last!
Cradling him.
Surrounding him!

Rays and shards from layers of
the sun... the sea... the sun!...

And... and... still there, over his shoulders...
... his Lycée... Abdelmalek al Saadi:
with its YEAR-LONG, blood-red Canac flowers...
Warm breath
From the Sahara.

The innocence of a Prediluvian setting
That does not yet, *know* snow!

Omni-present spiritual guides:
Like André Gide and Albert Camus:

The alchemy of Synesthesia, for the latter.

The *Disponibilité* of the body, for the former.

Zig-zag of shy, Mediterranean *pinède-scented calanques.*
Stonewalls, hand-cut by men before the first millennium.

He thought to himself:
"God... or the gods, must have had a favorite marble:
And this blue-one was it!"

And now,
his mind takes him back to that New England, *frozen field:*
Two teens... unaware of the cold.
Rolling in the snow... in the dark.
Humid breath coming from both.

And later... but only later... did he include,
in his lyrical description of the moments:
the Reality... of that *uneven presence...*
of the solidity of stones...
under them.

For a few precious and alchemic seconds,
Things. Time.... and pain did not exist:

But, **unlike** the *Nausée* of Sartre...
... in that dangerous crisscrossing of humanity and consciousness...
He did not fall... he *could not* fall into...
invasive... overwhelming materiality.

His consciousness ... **instead** of filling up
with philosophical emptiness...
filled itself instead,
-willingly, sensually and naturally-
With a contradictory mixture of deep-green Calvinism
and
Mediterranean-blue, bikini sunblock-balm.

With hints of Ricard Pastis
for his still unquenched-thirst for the Maghrebian landscape.

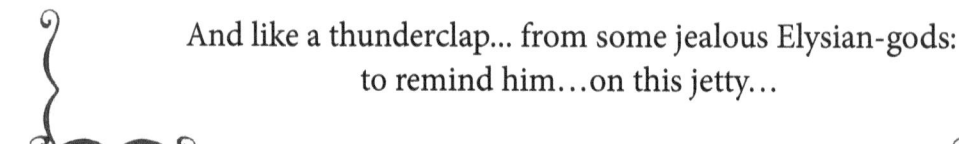

And like a thunderclap... from some jealous Elysian-gods:
to remind him…on this jetty…

of not only the Sartrean contradiction:
source of existentialist angst...
but also, the awareness that his Being...
could prosper *in emptiness*.

That both needed to exist:
Thanks to his very awareness... of **his** presence:
his **willing** embrace of this awareness.

His *human presence*...on that jetty
Still triggering a disturbance in the cloth of Things...
... by remaining grounded...
between the eternal beauty of the night sky
... and her.
Her...
... lying next to him on that field.

Allowing him, *unlike* Sartre... to feel at last...
at ease in the world of Things.

Things having been *witnesses* of that first kiss.
The First glance.

The yellow streaks of mimosas, on the hills,
overlooking the Mediterranean, on that late winter day:

Bornes-les-Mimosas
and her voluptuousness integrated into the flora...
like a reclining, Matisse nude .

Taking satisfaction, in the solid reassurance from things...
...that his beloved Provence...
would **continue in the solidarity**
of someone else's passion.

Unlike Roquentin's, darkish existentialist reaction …
he believed in the redeeming power of human lyricism.

From his apparent innocent playtime of his youth,
he remembered…
the attractive, corrupted image of this venomous African viper
that had invaded his hide-away
in the eucalyptus forest.

Even after many years later
-dangerously late in adulthood-
and contrary to a purely Sartrean,
cerebral reaction…
he remembered, instead "a quasi-erotic, sensual frisson"
to that snake.

The strangely, **pleasant** acridity of the eucalyptus leaves
had **perfumed** his memory.

The snake never had a chance!
The author was saved from a biblical Fall:

No descent into Sartre's Nausea!

In this tale…
the writer's feeling is more at ease in the world.

As for the haphazard of contingency:
That takes all **meaning or purpose** away…
…. to him, it opened to possibilities…
to hedonism…. to the senses
Even if… it is in front of a blind… dumb… and deaf…
meaningless contingency.

Glorious Return to Paris

Glorious return to Paris …

    Welcomed through whiffs of instants:
       blissfully scattered over Paris.

         Still warm:
    t*hrobbing* from the cobblestones.
       Visceral tremors.

       Deep-throated,
      mutual acquiescence.

    Sensual *call of the wild*:
Echoes… unheard in years, for their ears!

      Remnants of scenes,
first viewed through the striation of eye-lids.

    Vagueness... of heavenly softness
       of lumpy mattress.

    Limitless expanse of hours.
      And space.... space!
      Miraculous space!
In this, seventh-floor, miniscule, converted maid's chamber.

      Pieces of languages:
    Half French. Half English.
    -of intermingled identities-

The magic... of flesh...
... somehow...
managing to concretize indescribable seconds.

Akin to incantations...
-from priestesses and priests in translucent-nakedness-
in smoky temples

The arc of their lives:
seemingly, lost in the debris of things.

And then...
these ghostly, smiling apparitions
-in the corner of the room-
as though *approving-spirits of former Parisian lovers:*

The city, tempting souls again:
-by honoring them-
while reconstructing the *reality of dreams.*

To the music of "Best of Tropical Deep House Music Chill House Summer Mix 2022".

A Virility in Her Voice

Attempted redemption, of an otherwise perfect soul.

    Waiting for his time in the faculty room.
        -at the mimeograph machine-

Escapist visions taking over his thoughts.

    The dead weight of routines,
        drowning his present.

    Mindless, witty banter of his remarks
        -impressing the co-ed audience-
    about his activities for the coming week...
        ... and then ...
the *virility* of a **new** voice behind him.

    As... of yet... a faceless voice...
    in a register of ambivalent sexuality.

    Like some of the passages of his syllabi,
he tried to interpret this addition to his *reality*...

    "Reading the literary tea-leaves":
He would often propose to his classes.

And thus,
Greek oracles and deities!
Vaporous vestals!...
.... appeared in the drab confines of the tiny cinderblock office!

Jean-Yves Vincent Ciccariello Solinga

He hesitated turning around:
Somehow... uncontrollably and correctly
fearing a fatal bohemian tug
on his bourgeois soul.

———

Like those pivotal moments:
found in the pages of biblical accounts of humanity's
classical luminaries and sinners.

Moments, like those of the inhabitants of Paradise:
shielding their eyes in their naked shame!

Fatidic moments,
that make you instinctively cover your glance
at the sight of you fate.

———

So... He knew... He knew! ....
well before sealing his inevitable and predictable Fall,
with his Faustian... all too human, very earthy attraction to pleasures...
... he willingly entered...
... the *"Powdery concentration of hallucinatory happiness:
Beyond the bounds of existential ethics.
But not beyond the culpability from [his] ethics."****

*** *As he had put it: quoting his own writings. [Regarding, reality: invading art {in the fashion of "The Singing Detective"}]*

Wine in the Streets

"They poured wine in the streets": Headlines banners, under newspapers photographs of protesting Americans, to the United Nations', French Ambassador speech against Afghanistan's war involvement.

In some Gallo-centric circles... mistreating this liquid
would be akin to quasi-blasphemy!

The substance, present at the *Passion!*
Its presence of honor at sacred, family rites of passage!

———

The pedestal of pride as it is gently uncorked,
sniffed... reflected upon...
and endlessly debated.

Yes! That same glorious product!

Pride and joy of humanity, ever since,
its happenstance discovery
in a drunken taste:

Leftover grape juice,
on the hills and heat of some Greek island.

The same "leap forward"
akin to the lunar steps...

Some of us...
would gladly offer, our share,
to the gods of peace.

Jean-Yves Vincent Ciccariello Solinga

If ethereal intoxication,
could only erase the fear of imagined
weapons of mass destruction.

Thus, redeeming the lonely, diminutive figure
of Dominique de Villepin
in the enormous United Nation Hall.

Weapons into Plowshares

To the memory of D.D., killed [early 1970's] in a skirmish in the jungle of Cambodia: he was in his early twenties.

Average student, from quaint New England village:
He had regularly been deposited at the high school
-at the top of the hill-
by yellow school bus.

Maybe, not so much interested in multiple-choice exams,
in order to garner a prized college deferment:
he garnered, instead, an M 16.

———

In the surrealist universe of
flexible alternatives or temporal possibilities.
Realities...
... could have, instead, landed him
on this air-craft carrier.

Into this college basketball-game rivalry. **
On this exquisite war-machine.
Within splendid vistas of radiant sun.
Ocean breezes and infinity of blue horizon.

Instead,
of grabbing some errant grenade.

*** Gonzaga basketball game on U.S.S. Abraham Lincoln aircraft carrier.*

Weapons Designer

Yellow chalk on green board:
Trajectory of object in flight, versus gravity.

Teacher... capturing ephemeral moments in equations...
While... *He* would be furiously doodling
beautifully-finned Cadillac cars.

That was his love:
Lovingly encompass metal shapes
in the softness of number-three lead-pencils.

It had, even garnered, the approval of the sciences teacher: Mister D...
... when apprehended red-handed!

"You'd better earn a living... drawing cartoons...
... because, beautiful cars are not sciences!"

———

And earn a good living... he did.
His innate skills, spotted early as a draftee for Viet Nam:
He designed the most efficient
Anti-personnel weapons.

This might have explained his somber silence,
when they met, for a beer,
upon their return from "Nam".

(1960's College-track sciences class) He sat next to him in physics class: elegantly intelligent and high emotional quotient. He never could understand his career-choice acquiescence.

Lifeless Glance

Newsreel of a defeated German soldier, walking through the obliterated, former elegance of a Berlin boulevard... looking straight at the camera.

Did the decrescendos and crescendos;
Teutonic overtones of the Führer;
his near-whispers...
followed by canine barks of delusional anger...
still haunt him?

Was the diminutive, slander figure at the lectern,
still shouting to spellbound seas of green sticks?

Did the sounds still reverberate in this soldier's mind...
as his disheveled head looked into the camera?
Did it?
Did the musical sound of exquisite waltzes...
the divine virility of Wagnerian phrasing?
Did it?
Which parts...
of the splendid accomplishments from this gem of a culture....
-itself on the crown of the evolved tip of Western Europe-
... what shreds of all of these memories...
... did come forth, in this non-helmeted man?
.... maybe the doubt...
"Was it worth it?"

Time Started…

Time started… when the universe
-in its unconscious pieces-
Continued…
In its unconscious way.

Time continued,
When one of the pieces, of this universe… moved away from another.

When changes… blindly
Imposed themselves on the primordial soup.

When THAT piece, flying away from the rest
-created the first differentiation-
… between here… and there!

The first Greek-DELTA signature.

That became…NOW… and the other… some other time.

―――――

Our silicon-dust brain,
Somehow having acquired the sensing-ability
For that difference.

Our humanity… as we sense it… being the result.

Such things as…
World War One and its dead.
Being…
Or not… ever…having been.

Beautiful arabesques of astrophysics,
Made of white chalk:
Of no value to the equation,
Except… for its symbolic state…
…as dust… on the professor's shoes.

Unexpectedly heartbreaking confession by incredibly gifted student, in highly regarded university.

Visiting Daddy at Work

Sternness of impenetrability of black, shiny leather jacket...
His arms, wrapping, so gently...
the flowery waves of her cotton dress.

Microcosm of peaceful fatherly love.
Perfect balance of contradictory forces of this world:
A menacing Glock 17s for one...
And her favorite pastel blankie.

Spontaneity... of the classic pose and forces:
Brutal energy... and the innocence of unsoiled emotions.

All... in perfect balance for a precious moment
And a tearful goodbye... going home.

Strength. Protection.
And unconditional tenderness...

For both to share:
Imprinted unto their souls...
Safe there... and forever-after.

Strength. Protection.
And unconditional love.

Photograph of a police officer-dad, in full gear, next to NYPD squad car, on Times Square: holding his daughter, on a visit... "where daddy works".

Under the Skin

His stature among us
did not have to be verbalized:
We never had to label him our leader.

His unassuming self-assuredness,
gave an uncommon, ethical solidity to our social rituals:
Unlike the many quasi-tribalistic nature of the dorm-parties,
He...
somehow, imparted a certain *nobility* to our evenings:
"Girls... simply... felt safe"... with him, in our mist.

———

She,
appeared... one Saturday night:
Seamlessly becoming associated with him.
And... no vote
was needed to recognize them as the perfect couple.

And then... the end of academic life:
Commencement. The draft. The hunt for 4F status.
And parents' goals to satisfy.

Entries, in the proverbial list of dates "black-books", had to be crossed off.
The betterment of individual, sedate futures... *obliged*.

———

And so, he revealed,
-seated on a lumpy bed and warm beer in hand-
that higher orders of the soul had destroyed those of his heart.

That night... in that dorm-room
-In full spectrum of suffering of emotional agonies-

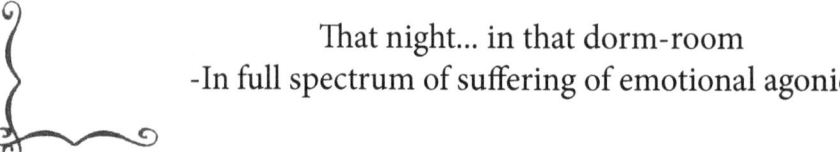

He confessed his hopeless love:
A marginal girl: a "local-drop out!"

Inserting, into the mundane of his life,
our numerous, abstract, late-night discussions of textbooks:
"The classical dilemma in Greek tragedies."

Very close, university friend's confession, in high-end, private New England college room. Attractive qualities in this "man's man". Endless potential. With destructive, classical situation: Falling in love with local girl, from an impoverished town.

"I can't introduce her to my parents. And, I have her under the skin!"

Unrepentant *Humanist* in the Entrails of an M.R.I. **

Oh! the uncanny... uncontrollable...
human ability of consciousness!

In the infernal entrails of the M.I.R.
... and yet, this quaint temerity of challenging the *machine*.

He tries to settle himself.
Tries to find a purpose and meaning to the chaotic noise.

———

Appropriately and practically naked.
Protected by only one's skin.

Biological delusions...
from his mind:
Like the rooster of medieval fables,
thinking his crowing wakes up the sun!

———

He has to make sense of the infernal pounding.
Antihuman. Non-human cacophony!!

As though some evil force had set the metronome
... to the cosmological meter-beat!

———

As proof of courage:
Attempting to sleep,
to spite the inhuman rhythms and notes of dissonance.

No matter the best efforts of the built-in silicon circuitry
-Programed or unprogrammed-

of this damn machine:
... here he lies, in glorious, noble hospital gown!

Now...able... no!... inspired!
... in capturing shards of lyricism...
from the dumb, code-driven noise.

Finding phrasing. Unity of sounds.
Rhythmic repetitions.
Sympathetic echoes. Accidental harmony.

Hints of sanity.... in this enclosed tunnel.

The glorious arrogance.
The unmitigated arrogance: the imposition of the *sentient mind*.
And, somehow... re-creating a symphony of modicum beauty...

... out of the brutish dissonance and emotional void.

Inspired by an M.R.I. experience. **
"For the composer... dissonant... atonal music... gave the freedom of sounds among sounds; as the periodic table, accorded the chemist the rearranging of atoms among atoms, for the pleasure and need of instinctive, human need for new order... new understanding... and new placement." One of the more succinct definition/description of the revolutions [starting, as far back as Mozart] in musical writings. From another Cognac-lubricated conversation.

** *Surrealistic sounds, unrelated bangs... knocks... machine-grunts... etc... in no less than a stereophonic headset, inside the stainless-steel tube of an M.I.R.*

To the "Smooth Sounds of Mr. Paul Hardcastle and Helen Rogers Sunshine"[first cut on replay]

To that Unknown Soldier…

[from an English version of Les Misérables]
The Bishop: *Now don't forget, don't ever forget, you've promised to become a new man.*
Jean Valjean: *Promise? What, why are you doing this?*
The Bishop: *Jean Valjean, my brother, you no longer belong to evil. With this silver, I have bought your soul. I've ransomed you from fear and hatred, and now I give you back to God. (Les Misérables [Victor Hugo])*

Did he feel like a reluctant modern-day King Solomon?
Among the heady swirls of geo-politics…
this intimate family tragedy…
with all the added, classic anguish of maternal love.

Unavoidable tears, playing on an unforgiving stage
of raw…sanguine emotions.

Seating behind a spartan military-style office
-of World War Two inspiration-
his double-silver bars, reflecting the morning sun.

An unenviable, recurrent dilemma
between bureaucracies and clean consciences.

Imposition of godly powers…
… on mere humans.

That lonely status of feeling like a single cog
in the infernal machinery of wars.

The daily need for new flesh
and its contemplated weight in individual mourning.

Godly demands on this one man:
Unsought and unwanted.

The glaring, easy temptations
-of still empty check-off boxes-
to appease… both compliant, or guilty consciences.

Literatures and mythologies,
showing the way to transpose the weighty decision to the next column.

Because, either way, that Monday night,
that officer would have been served his free supper.

There was no entry for *humanism* in the questionnaire.
No one would need to know:
Wife, children or next career… no one.

A magnanimous, silent and solitary act:
Humanity's antidote… to a blind, dumb…
… and cold cosmos.

Story told, from the next bar-stool and boozy haze, of army basic training captain, at the height of the Viet Nam war, conscription is at its highest. Upon returning to his barrack (after seeing his dying father) a distraught, AWOL soldier's future is in the hands of this lanky officer who signs the form that made possible an honorable discharge:

Kafka... Revisited

The T.S.A. officer, did what some... fear the most:
And yet, for practically anyone else...
... just a simple hesitation.

Innocuous movements of the head:
Left to right. Up and down. And back.

But for him...
... in the fraternity of similar others,
... in the pages of the injustices imposed by their birthplace...
It said it all:
"What is This?... Your first name?..."

And then the fall into the bottomless depth of bureaucracy.
Helplessness of the body and the mind.

Capriciousness of the next hours and days.
Multiple past lives... mangled.
Futures... changed.
Like...
like... that last glance upon your little brother.

―――

Unspeakable injustices imposed on sentient life
-Because *sentient*-
And, its very awareness of the end of human bonds.

International departures... [from American customs officer]: " Your older sister's papers have a different spelling in French!?."

Jamestown Revisited

Across the *North Atlantic* and then… across the Cosmos…

Scientists and philosophers, ethicists and programmers,
will have scrubbed, like some insidious bedbug,
the memory-banks of artificial intelligence.

Thus, high-grade filters,
proactively protecting the cosmos from earthlings' classical flaws.

Humans are coming!
These creatures so susceptible to bacterial infection…
and yet… inventors of gods.

———

The dangers of travel,
will still have been in the prosaic details.

Those wrapped in our luggage
and forgotten under our pajamas.

The mythology of our mythologies:
Found in well intentioned sermons:
as well as political bile.

Our neurons, still arrogantly *reflecting upon themselves*:
The dangers of a third rail…
Faustian knowledge…
Under the guise of an apple-tree in a *Paradise!*

We wanted… we needed to see behind doors!
Beyond the limits of our village.
Beyond the seen and unseen.

And so, we will, unavoidably, have brought along
Our combined best and worst:
Our majestic humanism and puny carnality.

Everything, about everything, symbolically played
among the waving reeds of an August day
in a *new world*...

... Untold freedom... space... and misery.

On August 20, 1619, first enslaved Africans arrive in Jamestown, setting the stage for slavery in North America: Brought in by the Portuguese, to the British colony of Virginia who are then bought by English colonists. Nota bene: the irony of international cooperation.

Just Some Syllables

Observing a couple, recognizing each other's name, in a busy train station.

How could, just three syllables...
Three distinct sounds in the cacophony of the train station...
How could the oral fluidity of her name,
remind him of its far-away, Hawaiian-island origin?

He was simply immobilized...
petrified ... .incapable of turning around:
his body, reverting to an incarnation of proto-humanity,
deep in the muds of creation.
Myths must have been constructed this way:
In order to impose our visions on *things*.

These two lovers... now...
Transposed into a cocoon of silence of nuptial whispers:
Completely oblivious to the mob of passengers.

Their very quasi-statuesque immobility...
somehow, imposed an instinctive and natural reaction...
as a respectful flow opened around them!

It must have happened in the infancy of this very particular need, and increasing ability, for humans to communicate: maybe driven by a perfect balance of procreative-drive and the first warm Spring-evening around their Mediterranean grotto... pointing to a radiant flower and repeating the "sound" for "it" toward a female... that SHE [her face, her presence] had "acquired"... the rich fluidity of those syllables, that easily flowed off his lips. The rest is lyrical history and would... oh, so naturally... repeat itself in a Nineteenth Century Paris train station.

Jean-Yves Vincent Ciccariello Solinga

Returning From the Atrocities of War

Thinking about the delusional bravado of former soldiers "fond memories of their military days" and that of a mother.

Ex-colleagues,
seemingly unaffected by military savageries.

Impeccable respect for civil order:
Not a speeding tickets in sight.

Irreproachable moral standards,
reinforced every Sunday:

Postcard-perfect lives and living.

For one...
hushed hints and rumors
of special-forces hand to hand combat.

Virility of aggression as demanded.

Primordial survival as required
in bloodied, muddy swamps.

Miraculously,
still attached to a sensitive soul.
......
For the other...
... endless references to meteoric rise in ranks:
linked to the chemical effectiveness
... of Agent Orange.

Heartbreaking viewing images of a mother, in subway, with her children.

Noilly Prat

Resulting crescent of a fertile world,
at the confluence of synesthesia and the reconstruction of the past.

All too familiar... seemingly antithetical pieces of memories.

Symbiosis of paternal love... kitchen-table rituals...
... all gently wrapped in the hue of an ideal youth.

Doctor visits and parental teary eyes...
... leading to the daily appearance of these brittle, glass-ampoules:
Smartly snapped open, between index and thumb.

Repulsive bitterness of miraculous,
life-saving vitamin supplement... appropriately intermingled
with the herbal, alchemic essence of Provençal fields.

Medically prescribed glass-ampoules of necessary supplement, smartly mixed with Noilly Prat, red-Vermouth wine.

A Nihilist's Fervent Wish

Another, Cognac-driven, parlor game. Question: "What would be your wish in your nihilist world?"

For those for whom, the idea of a Garden of Paradise,
had died long ago, in still-birth.

A place, where any chance of
good or bad... ethical or perverted...
were evenly boring.

What momentary joy!
A sliver of justice!

———

Such as... a fervent hopeful wish, on the part of a suicidal Hitler **
-with his trembling Luger-
CRYING...
... at the fleeting echoes of his mother's voice.

A universe where... the organic simplicity...
of the voice of one's mother,
would not be asphyxiated in cosmic dust.

———

Instead, we find ourselves in an absurdist play:
driven by Einsteinian mathematical formulae.

With only... our human-imposed, *pleasurable* intermissions,
in the lobby.

[** *The reader is free to substitute her/his favorite face of Evil.*]

A Place That Only Exists in Poetry
A fable

Religious chronicles of Arabian-peninsula western expansion [El-Maghreb], reaching the expanse of the Atlantic Ocean: an obstacle to proselytizing.

Enraged!...
he had his horse buck...
making it, kick his front legs over the edge of the cliff.

Flashes in his mind...
of places, people and cultures to subjugate.
And this windy, *obstinate* vastness... of greenish ocean...
stopping his troops!

―――

Visions of the little boy... from the dry desert that he was...
invaded his soul!

The very same youngster,
playing *explorer* and *conqueror* in the surrounding hills.
... places, people and cultures to convert!

Playing the protagonists of his school tales.

―――

Glancing down... to his right side...
The majestic man... on his majestic horse...
saw a mother's fearful glance in a *young shepherdess'* eyes...
... and went home...

A slightly, surrealistic thought-experiment, of un-calculable results due to a haphazard, arbitrary change, in a pivotal historic event: in this case, a change of heart, of an unquestioned leader, provoked by the glance of a mother's fears.

An untethered, fanciful and benign rewriting -by the author- ... of all and any... of the belligerent tales of religious and cultural human expansions in history chapters.

A Lyrical Incursion into Her Sexuality

Inspired by the mixture of topics: political theories and unbridled sexuality in "La philosophie dans le boudoir [Philosophy in the Bedroom by le Marquis de Sade]

A lyrical incursion into her sexuality.
A descent... into organic meanders, full of protective defenses.

Literary themes
often inserted into their conversations.

-Part of their mutual interests in academia-

They had spent respective years
plowing the richness of human unease.

Cultured places,
in the created worlds of things and people.

Chaotic spaces contaminated, at times, with the most
irreligious... the depraved.

Tears from the sentient awareness
of humanity's orphaned-status.

All...
intelligently analyzed and categorized.
-In their respective, literary niches-

All, part of humanity's inexcusable knowledge
-In a post-paradisiac world-

Taking over for their gods.
Being now,
their own architects.

Of morality ...guilt... innocence.

-In life. Living. Stages and tragedies-

And then...
this recurring question about a *particular adventure*.
And amidst the whiteness of the sheets...
this transfixing... dark glance...
....

To the music of Paul Hardcastle, Helen Rogers – "Sunshine".

Jean-Yves Vincent Ciccariello Solinga

A Mother's Tomato-Dressing

*Rue des écoles, (Port Lyautey) Kénitra, Morocco (1959) [with poetic license].
Noontime lunch with my mother, in her tax office.*

Functional drabness of a tax office:
Assortment of multi-levels of folders:
All containing various dry stages, of mundane miseries.

And yet... at that moment... and to this day...
the pure... insulated passion, of precious *moments*.

The setting... now, more a sacred ceremonial:
with its incense from perfumed tomatoes.

Specks of these priceless seconds of youth:
still filtering the mineral edges of reality,
through a mesh of tender filigree.

Brown... school, leather, book-bag:
lazily leaning against the wall.

She would have moved, another chair, to her desk.

———

Intoxicating intensity
of deep-green basil from my father's garden.

Pungency of silky oils, from plump garlic...
once more, invading my nostrils.

The alchemy of lyricism, still penetrating
the boundaries of sleepy, adult wisdom:

Letting the soul, take refuge,
from the frigid New England, February night...
into the mimosas of youth.

A successful attempt at reaching the Holy Grail of lyricism: the emotional "Singularity" of mind and body senses.

Neanderthal Man in Charge

How would you explain... to a Neanderthal man
-that upon the closure of the paradisiac gates-
He would, eventually,
be left in charge of Earth?

Or what a driver in Manhattan is doing in this yellow metal box?

The separation between machine and emotion
-or its equivalent-
having long ago incestuously intermingled into a singularity?

The construction -reconstruction-
Of love.
Time.
Moments.
The future.

Showing, a first-century shepherd from Bethlehem, videos
of the practical, historical consequences of his dead son?

How Greek tragedies were staged preambles
to the harsh realities of coming World Wars?

Painting magic that would bring the heat of the sun
and the collective obedience of sun flowers
-from the field of Aix-en-Provence-
viscerally to the museum viewer.

Pathos needs susceptibility of the spirit.

But what if, upon turning things forever over to us…
What if (God) [sic] … had had pangs of guilt?

His last glance...
watching us destroying the globe.

Thus, living us, instead with the cosmic generated glimmers of hope
that our human body-machine
would self-generate the will... the means...
... to teach itself restrain or wisdom.

Otherwise,
nothingness will turn back into nothingness.

Cognac-driven conversation between defrocked-priest from Paris Saint-Sulpice and former American draft-dodger, in back-street café of Quartier Saint Michel: Topic of the "apéritif"... God has turned the keys over to us.

Of Kisses Under the Bridges of the Seine

Juliette Gréco and Miles Davis meeting each other at the Salle Pleyel in Paris, 1949.

Poets... and other dreamers believe
in the transcendental power and visceral nature
of mere human emotions.

Emotions...
that... in some of our more privileged moments,
are capable of provoking jealousy, in our gods.

These sleepy, divine, museum figures:
coming down, and out, of their static, museums displays.

Full of rage and envy toward us
mere humans:
as they witness this apparently common affliction
... love!

A mundane encounter, in the wings of a jazz concert...
and nothing more...
than glances into the *other's* eyes.

An unverbalized... sensual invitation... into someone else's soul:
without the artifice -or need- for a common language.

An idyll beyond time and space.
A place beyond the organic.

Beyond Segregation and skin pigmentation.
Beyond drug addiction.

Amidst the existential angst of the Left Bank.

Turning the "quais de la Seine"
into their private nuptial cocoon.

Lyricism... found at the intersection of musical virility
and the supple tenderness of *knowing* lips
against the mouthpiece.

Joined by the deep femininity of a cabaret voice.

The *beauty of an Egyptian god*,
at its genesis.

Jean-Paul Sartre [to Miles Davis]... "Why don't you get married to Juliette Gréco...". Miles Davis [to Sartre]... "because I love her too much."

["Egyptian god" Juliette Gréco's description of her first impression of Miles Davis]

Tickets Only

Aéroport de Nice, Côte d'Azur.

At the... "Passengers-with-tickets-only" sign:
It was over.

It could not continue... or restart.
He knew it... she knew it.
It would only rekindle the hurt again.

―――――

But he had to *say* something insightful.
Deep.
He felt, she half-expected it from him.

He had gone over several drafts of beautiful lyrical sentences.

―――

All he could say,
as he crumpled the note in his pocket:
as she kissed him ... and started turning around
while *she kept silent* was...
"I will never fall in love the same way".

"I think, I know now, what I mean, in my classes, by...
love refashions your heart."

Nineteenth-Century literature professors, personally living... silently and passively, in their academic world.

Jean-Yves Vincent Ciccariello Solinga

Musical Odyssey

Inspired by "Kashmir "by Led Zeppelin

Echoes and smells of the of Medina des Oudaias.**
Huge ocher-mud wall
Jealously protecting this exotic space
Sensual confusion of smells
Hypnotic effects of heat
and musical repeated drumming
of instruments
attraction of guttural sounds
the seemingly endless sinuous alleys
full of questions and questionable dead-ends
everything and anything
seemingly exploding at once
from everywhere
memory of squeezing my father's huge hands
and letting it go… for the instant thrill
of the other side…
quasi-psychedelic trip
through confusion about the purpose of these attractive copper object

Visual stimulation of earliest flights into the other side
Quasi trepidation…

Perfect metaphor for an avatar of mortal sin,

Enormous abyss between the biblical fall in this land
of youthful innocence

Acrid whiffs of hashish
and suffocating turmeric powders

Grounded by my father's hand

To a fast-diminishing world

*** The author's first and most precious memories, are of the huge walls of the kasbah des Udayas: across the street from his house… and the hypnotic, rapid, musical drum-beat and especially the intoxicating flute [nair] floating from the Souk!*

The Voices of Angels

Waking up from surgery, amidst the background of indistinguishable [predominantly feminine] conversations of nursing staff.

It was the "tabla rasa" nature of the moment:
Like wearing the skin of a new born!

Some special status of the human mind:
The one... starting from an unformed
... an un-knowing... disconnected...
... consciousness.

An ideal *awareness* ...
with which to enter new worlds.

A particularly privileged and rare state:
All senses!
And no references!

All senses!
And yet... none of the naturally, life-long.-acquired filters!
All... and any opportunities,
apparently within reach.

A complete sensuality of unrestrained availability
of the body and a willing flesh.

———

But, the 'adult' grown up instincts
need to make sense of *things*.

Cradling softness underneath?
Warmth of heated towels?
The unrecognizable cold of sterile, neon-lights?

An then, the hurtful truth
of germs and diseases.

The background of chorus girls:
gathering sun-flowers, next to *Les Baux de Provence*.

A place of gentle conversation.
Idyllic setting.

And vestals preparing a danse!

Feeling safe!
Except, for the semi-nakedness of a hospital gown.

Waking up, in post-surgical administration of "Michael Jackson's milk"... Propofol, admits a pleasant background of mostly women's voices in the operating block, confused with chirping birds.

The Simplicity of Happiness

"I leave Sisyphus at the foot of the mountain. One always finds one burden again. But Sisyphus teaches the higher fidelity that negates the gods and raises rocks. He too concludes that all is well. This universe henceforth without a master seems to him neither sterile nor futile. Each atom of that stone, each mineral flake of that night-filled mountain, in itself, forms a world. The struggle itself toward the heights is enough to fill a man's heart. One must imagine Sisyphus happy." Albert Camus, Le mythe de Sisyphe [The Myth of Sisyphus]

An innocuous form in her garden:
He had heard more noise from her squeaking wheel-barrow.

Tending, every season
-in this unhospitable part of New England-
to her last surviving flower.

Silent and determined each Spring
for the endless and doomed ritual,
in this corner of *things*.

He would fancy, observing in her,
a Sisyphean figure:
Crouched at her doomed labor.

High up, from his writing vista,
he reluctantly discovered...
-Toward this diminutive, self-guided, *earthly presence*-
... a certain envy of her relationship with *dirt*.

She died... the way she had lived:
Seamlessly and at ease.

Admits the undefined forces of the universe...
which he had tried to warn her about.

Nihilist, having enviously observed his apparently content neighbor in the garden... on News of her death.

The Shape of Clouds

Teaching a French culture class, with "Tous les visages de l'amour". ["She"** in the English version] by Charles Aznavour]

Trying to describe the *shape of clouds*:
Trying to capture the intersection of pure sound and ethereal beauty...

... in the Other's language and culture.

Breaking the codes...
down to the particles... the molecules of human expressions.
To where they magically reach a critical mass.

And then... the chain-reaction.
The words... the grammar... transcended:
Like teaching the individual danse movements.

And the instant when the student does it
On their own... free in space.

And the comment... from the back of the room:
"... I don't fully understand...
but I can feel it through the French words."

** *Defending the unmeasurable beauty [a sort of special dimension] of the original French lyrics [and not English] of this song to skeptical classes.*
"*Toi, si Dieu ne t'avait modeler/ Il m'aurait fallu te créer*": [*If God had not fashioned you/ I would have had to give you life* [Translation J-Y.S.] [lyrics Charles Aznavour]

A Cold Winter-Night

Where fate, religion and "Docteur Rieux"** meet.

A cold Winter night… somewhere in the Middle East
A girl… and already a woman… in some ways…
had been laboring.

Her companion
had set his carpenter's toolbox down by the entrance
A confused panic had followed him next to his mate.

Whimpers and whispers
came from the group of assembled women

An acrid warmth
rose in swirls of smoke from the center of stable.
Their God had seemingly set things in motion:
… as they all were resigned…
To let nature, decide on events.

———

The next minutes were full of fear,
Pain and blood.

Fate and religions…
Working in the mysterious sphere:
The quick action of a veteran matron,
An old abused soul… with no pretention to an after-life:
Her compassionate solution,
for *unwanted-conditions*,
affectionately known by the girls of the local bordello…

… as much as…
having saved many newborn.

And thus, for this breached-child,
Now, safely swaddled in his mother's arms.

Any hint of solemnity, of the scene, was lost
on the tired carpenter
and the farm animals.

The travelling merchants shared their meals
with the assembly.

-Disobeying standing military orders-
a roman soldier, a new father himself,
distracted a search patrol: on the prowl for
some *predicted Messiah*.

Gold coins from an emotional businessman.
Were left in the hay of the manger.

This hillside creche was some sort of stage, for complete strangers,
to do human... basic... things.

In an avant-garde theatre of the Absurd,
Where various "actor-rebels"
Were on stage... and for a few fleeting minutes:
Mere mortals, managing to change the trajectory of an empty universe
At least ... for a night.

... with the fate of a *religion* in the balance.

Average humans... in a human world... managing to do... godly things.

*** Docteur Rieux of "la Peste" [the Plague] by Albert Camus.*

Artists Swallowed by Their Universe

To Camille Claudel, Arthur Rimbaud and Jimi Hendrix

Reality invaded them:
Cosmic *nuptials* as the go-between.

Willingly
possessed by the world and their world.

Capitulating to forces
that enter body and mind.

The creative act
being *THE* moment par excellence:
Since some hirsute hominid
Submitted.
Capitulated... to the need.

———

Driven to manipulating
layers of red mud on the cave walls.

Nuptials...
of all ... and any true artist since then.

Bringing together artists
and their projection of things...

An asexual act of submission...
-often in solitary silence-
for the unverbalized pleasure of others.

No artifice. No posing.
The artist:
-a sort of sacrificial lamb, before its day-

Finding some human redemption in the privilege
of non-verbal communication.
Honoring the artist's time on this earth:
too often sacrificed on the altar of their creativity.

The Death of Some Trees

"You blew it up! Ah, damn you! God damn you all to hell!" **

We will have done it:
Like underserving, spoiled teenagers...
Vomiting on your mother's best rugs.

Unappreciative of Grama's handmade table-top:
the one with the grandchildren's initials:
Now, with cigarette scars.

The broken front door:
that had welcomed all three new-births.

Life and living, among these walls,
on this side of this street...
had indeed been an island of privilege.

Symbol of consistency.
A place of solidity among the familiar and mundane.
This home,
one of the exceptional *things*... from an otherwise uncaring...
... silent universe.

This celebrating horde of youths,
mistaking the apparent subservient, deep-green silence,
as a signed-permission slip.

And drunken celebration...
with little awareness, that the *reddish* mud in the freshwater,
would be a prelude to a Martian landscape.

** Charlton Heston's character in the "Planet of the Apes" and the evidence of irreversible damage to the Amazonian basin.

A Last Sumptuous Meal

Place du Havre, Paris.
"Red wine with my fish"...
It was THIS... the ultimate insult:
This... the real negation of a well-lived, cultured life.

This apostatic statement:
Violating his status among the fragile border
between the dullness, homogenized consistency of our animal ancestry:
Found at the confluence of cosmic dust clumps... and their evolution
into our consciousness of things.

The quasi-miraculous leap...
... of our having an intellectual inkling
of what *is life*... and its opposite.

———

Such *moments*...
With the background sound of the bells
from les Saints Augustins church.

The crying wetness of Parisian sidewalks.
The nervous energy of impeccably dressed *serveurs*.

And ... as only human construct can define it...
... the "Anticipated Happiness"...
of mumbled moments.

It was not simply, knowing that he was witnessing a splendid example of a Parisian bon-vivant's "last sumptuous meal"... in the city's best table for that dish, across from la Gare Saint Lazarre... no... it was rather, that his family member's multi-decade, multi-pack smoking of unfiltered Gauloises and dementia, was still (instinctively?) fighting for his image... but really, breaking his heart in the process... with his insistence on a powerful, Bordeaux red with the establishment prized fish from the cold Atlantic... death [his friend would have agreed] would have been indeed, be more dignified for this Frenchman!

A *pre-Deified* Universe

Lifetime... deep infatuation with a senior academic figure.

Late to her Lecture...
She literally *entered* his life through an unadorned classroom-door:
Inauspicious apparition...
of bookish energy:
A tangle of luxuriant, rebellious black hair.

———

It was her *apparent* skill at dissecting passions
in the pages of tragedies.

A surgical dexterity
that laid bare, the nexus of human frailties at their limits.

The dichotomy between the intimacy of personal anguish.
Their historical, and epoch-changing impact.
In royal and common bloodline.

She somehow made it possible to imprint *seamlessly*
this universe of the stage on daily life.

———

Was it for having known them?
Or having acquired an immunity to emotional pain?

Was she like, these tragic Grecian figures:
petrified for the viewer?

Thus now, this wiser and older surviving soldier!

Having refused to re-enter another fray?
... by refusing his ouvertures?

And then to his astonishment, her showing him a window
into... *the world of a little girl...*
.....
... a world made of the raw... virginal, pre-paradisiac beauty
of the unseen and unwitnessed...
the natural... in its natural state.

A pre-deified universe...
Dangerously... gloriously independent of humanity's edicts.

The value, in such a 'private soul", of her declaration concerning her complicated past.

Magical Sandwich

A whole culture in a sandwich

He mindlessly had taken a bite of his sandwich...
and felt a disconnection in his being...

... the flavors in his nostrils
somehow at odds with his surroundings.

Still drowning in the verbal chaos of the *new language*.
As well as... now... feeling alienated ...
from the familiarity of the "cantine of his école primaire".

He had just experienced, something like an uncontained escape
of... and from... his very flesh.

An *unexpected* reconstruction took place
effortlessly... feeling dumfounded...
with a *revealed* awkwardness of tactile presence, in this foreign cafeteria.

He could envision *his mother's* approving smile
... of his awe...
at the quasi-alchemic nature, generated this *maternal gesture*.

Merciless ribbing, by American classmates, of new, high school student: an immigrant whose mother would make for him, her "Mediterranean-style" sandwiches. Circa 1950's, New England town, with very few available "European" ingredients: she had one day, [probably out of frustration] concocted a mixture of white cream-cheese, dry basil, thyme, rosemary and sprinkled olive oil, on Italian bread: The rest of the lunch table, usually eating an assortment of sliced, white-bread, peanut-butter and some sort of jelly/ marshmallow fluff-ware.

Jean-Yves Vincent Ciccariello Solinga

A Virility in Her Voice

Attempted redemption, of an otherwise perfect soul.

Waiting for his time in the faculty room.
-at the mimeograph machine-

Escapist visions taking over his thoughts.

The dead weight of routines,
drowning his present.

Mindless, witty banter of his remarks
-impressing the co-ed audience-
about his activities for the coming week...
... and then ...
the *virility* of a new voice behind him.

As... of yet... a faceless voice...
in a register of ambivalent sexuality.

Like some of the passages of his syllabus,
he tried to interpret this addition to his *reality*...

"Reading the literary tea-leaves":
He would often propose to his classes.

———

And thus,
Greek oracles and deities!
Vaporous vestals!...
.... appeared in the drab confines of the tiny cinderblock office!

Black Butterfly Dust

He hesitated turning around:
Somehow... uncontrollably and correctly
fearing a fatal bohemian tug
on his bourgeois soul.

———

Like those pivotal moments:
found in the pages of biblical accounts of humanity's
classical luminaries and sinners.

Moments, like those of the inhabitants of Paradise:
shielding their eyes in their naked shame!

Fatidic moments,
that make you instinctively cover your glance
at the sight of you fate.

———

So... He knew... He knew! ....
well before sealing his inevitable and predictable Fall,
with his Faustian... all too human, very earthy attraction to pleasures...
... he willingly entered...
... the *"Powdery concentration of hallucinatory happiness:*
Beyond the bounds of existential ethics.
But not beyond the culpability from [his] ethics."***

*** *As he had put it: quoting his own writings. [Regarding, reality: invading art {in the fashion of "The Singing Detective")]*

Jean-Yves Vincent Ciccariello Solinga

All the While...

All the while...
he had been reconstructing *moments:*

Humanity's source of pride and joy...
and the sweet-sour ambivalence, caused by the awareness of *time.*

The very *human-sourced* genesis of unverbalized,
instinctive needs.

Quasi animalistic:
as though, pre-ordained by some divinity.

A visceral genesis,
made of remains of our cosmic-dust.

———

It occurred to him, that her continuing... and very persistent existence...
Out of the realm of *things*... was all-encompassed,
in a miniscule pre-*Big Bang* space and time.

Every morsels of her being,
somehow impervious to dumb... unfeeling...
eternity.

And thus...
here she was... in her rich complexity and contradictions....
... here...
until the last drop... of *her favorite coffee.*

The cliffs of Sidi Moussa... revisited

And Humans "Constructed" the Universe

Like the rooster of the medieval fables: pretentiously thinking his crowing wakes up the sun.

A new graduate assistant.
A miniscule room, in multi-room, urban setting:

Looking over the typically-congested "Big Dig" traffic, three stories down.

He sighed to himself:
"I should have perfected my baseball swing!"...
... when summer reflections, of the night-games,
would seem to taunt him.

These caustic second-thoughts of career choices:
Seemingly diluted,
in the contact of the distilled water of his table-top analyses.

His designated training "partner"...
No less than a world-known researcher!

The better fairy tales
are made of unpretentious lessons.

Gently... humanly.
... "If we are honest with ourselves"...
[this eminent lab-partner, whispered]
" these life-saving proteins,
have been patiently waiting to be discovered!'

Early, hopeful results of vaccine research.

Artificial Dreams

"After some time... after the "Singularity", between humans and 'machines'... could there possibly exist... a virtual dreamscape of virtual corporal-synesthesia... that would appease humanity's, quasi-biblical, constant -and Faustian need- for knowledge and happiness?" [In "Notes of a personal mythology.]

Poets and dreamers...
long hindered by the bounds and limits of bodily flesh;
but apparently
still tempted by the shiny forbidden-apples of Paradise.

The ever presence and appeal of... knowledge...
... and knowledge, beyond knowledge.

Steamy spaces of...
conceived and conceivable spaces:
beyond sleepy and wise curiosity.

———

Finally appeasing these poets and dreamers!
These great sufferers of the retrains of normal evolution!

And still, all of these *eternal discontents of humanity!*

The... Arthur Rimbauds... of humanity's creativity!
These demanding artists and their kindred spirits...
with their artificial escapes... into artificial clouds of opiates.

Constantly, attempting to break earthly restrains!

———

And now... Yes!... the rescue of a future attraction:
A human singularity with *the machine*...
more likely, bringing a modicum of artistic freedom.

But happiness !? Human contentment !?

———

Would we have, probably, been better off...
... dying at the stage of the dinosaurs.

Naively looking up
at the increasing brightness of a giant, earth-killing meteor...
... munching on tender and tasty blades of grass?...

Jean-Yves Vincent Ciccariello Solinga

Between "Boogie Wonderland" and Reality

Lyrical speculations on Burt Reynolds' final visions

Was it the pleasurable drowning:
Asphyxiation by ingestion of hedonism?

Flashes of the concrete... the visceral:
Of apparently immortal instants.

Polyester, leisure-suit-clad figurine,
Having, accidently, transcended the mundane.

At the last stop of an earthy *life*:
Now,
ironically, attached to plastic tubing.

―――

Did he...
Uncontrollably.
With the natural of a *good-old-boy*:

-Outside of heady Einsteinian equations-

Not fully understanding his privilege?
Did he...
For an infinitely, short cosmic-instant, heroically
-and in spite of himself-
Stand...one foot... in the mud of time
and one
in the rarefied poetry of pleasure?

To the looped sound of Earth Wind and Fire" Boogie Wonderland.

Between Kabul and Kashmir

In homage to Jimmy Page and Robert Plant's lyrical voices: building beauty out of unhospitable, semi-desertic emptiness. (Moroccan Atlas and Kashmir mountains, iconic names that evoke quasi-mythological, desertous regions of armed conflicts)**

Knowledge of history: too often,
a predictable litany of preordained, nationalistic *destinies*.

Patriotic Pantheons of visionaries and demi-gods.
University-examinations, *blue*-books:
filled with regurgitated, pre-cooked ideas and ideals.

Beliefs and their opposites,
taking place in different nations, languages and cultures:
Self-assured of their unerring ways.

Panoply of civil and military deities and their iconic representations:
in museums, sturdy cathedrals and scented temples.

Engraved granite monuments:
in ethereal, peaceful, green prairies, overlooked by smiling clouds.

The whole infernal machinery,
fed by the humanity of its villages, regions, countries and continents.

All and everyone:
mothers and grandmothers…

… lovers…teachers and neighbors:
contributing to the cast of doomed characters.

All needed, in order to fill emotional, battlefield trenches:
across those of the enemy.

The eternal soldier... dying... eternally
on his concrete altar.

U.S. soldier, from rural Tennessee, crouched, under attack, looking up at the luxuriant, green canopy of the jungle. [in "Notes of a personal mythology": "I am the eternal soldier... sacrificed on an invisible altar."
["My kingdom is not of this world"... a line from an Army Chaplain's funeral-service sermon.]
** see various pages of "Sidi Moussa", Jean-Yves Vincent Ciccariello Solinga.

"Black-Folk" Cemetery

The battle of slogans: "Black lives matter"... classroom.... teacher... popular control and parent-prerogatives: trying to discuss and undo centuries of after-effects of slavery and racism.

She embodied,
under the sterile lights of the amphitheater...
the rich genesis of humanity's birth.

The echoes of visceral anger in her voice:
at that place where imagery is concretized.

The viewer felt exhausted.
The *spoken testimonial* was over.

The forgotten names on "black-folks" tombstones had been read.

An irrepressible feeling
of sacred reverence toward her "iconic" figure
in the middle of the stage.

He simply
wanted to genuflect in front of her transmutation...
into pages of humanism...

... and maternal presence.

She had just read "the name": adding that it was that of a three-year toddler taken from the slave-mother: a member of a wealthy New England, sea trader's household.

"Congolese Hell"

Article in "Journal Afrique"

Hellish irony...
... in the probable birthplace of human origins.

Evolutionary forces, having taken over...
our failed, early-cousins:
left "behind"
-in the roulette wheel of natural selection-

WE... somehow... seem to have deserved continuation.
The top of the heap... we are!

With all the trinkets of sentient awareness of ourselves.
And... *free will!*
-The complexity of inventing religions-

And thus... these rag-tag soldiers,
-Gri-Gri affixed to their biceps and machetes in hands-
... determining the religion of their next victims.

-In fields-
with bodies, in various state of putrefaction.

Like Poetry on Silk

The sender was a gentle soul:
His presence
among our pre-disillusioned quartet of draftees
was *de rigueur*:
"He belonged with us."

All of us:
College degree in hand… and M16 in the other.

The collective nightmare had concluded well enough for us:
"We had survived."

Images of horrors
Folded on the highest shelves of our closets.
With the bell-bottoms.

———

And then this attachment:
These decades later.

———

From our most endearing member:
The one, slightly stoned:
most of the time…

But "could he transform his visions
into layers of pastels!"

He had somehow managed to capture the tenderness
-of Debussy's *L'après midi d'un faune*-
On the natural pliability of silk:
With the cold efficiency of smart telephone!

A dormant canal along peaceful rice patties:
Former staging for death and dying.

And the cosmic irony
of the remains of church steeples, in the background…!

The recipients:
Our group of grumbling survivors:
Rewarded with an advance glance into heavens!

The completely unexpected photograph of a Vietnam canal around Hanoi: decades after the end of the war. [photograph, ironically, recently taken during the infamous "Tet" holydays].

Cultivating Our Gardens **

This "feeling" of a godlike infinity out there.
This void...
Humanly conceived and delineated.
This void...
Fully filled to the rim with our earthly worries.
This void...
Somehow connected to our birth.

All of it...
the driving force and inspiration
for a collective and intensely personal speculation.

Some intimately personal... some well-intentioned.
Visceral. Organic.

Splendidly-evolved neurons:
Chemically driven by results of evolution.

Impeccable upper-brain activities:
fertile fields for religious zealots.

Everything and everyone, invested
in clear answers from philosophy and philosophers.

With no cognitive matter
Floating throughout the nebulae
We manage to delude ourself... and others.

Comforting... yes.
Creative... yes.
The driving force and energy for good arts...
Spell-binding plays and acting.

Leaving us...
like Docteur Rieux, with the only thing that counts:
Our dealing with the *other things*
on this third planet.

** from "Candide" by Voltaire.
Of Voltaire, Kant and Camus: during another Cognac-driven discussion of these former philosophers, and their views on a... "Divinity, and its relationship to humanity".

Ode to the "Septic-Pumping" Business

Of the lessons of author's ancestral, Neapolitan history, with recurring-cholera epidemics.
Earthy interruption, from the lyrical world:
Flight-of-fancy prose,
about longing from the writer about some *Faustian-fever!*

And then…
this sinful disrespect, of superimposing
glistening piles of septic mud…

.. Over…
the maritime-pines…
the white, rocky Mediterranean-coast line.
And across *le Golf du Lion:*
the magic sorcery of magical-names:
Barcelona, Marseille, Genoa…
on the computer screen!

Disgusting, if it were not for family lore, about *ancestral*, Italian refugees,
from the magical beauty
of the notoriously polluted, bay of Naples:

And its cholera-infected children!

Personal reaction, upon viewing septic-tank cleaning, while writing poetry:
"Let us not forget that the earth self-recycles its global wastes!

Death in Paris

To the sound of "Paul Hardcastle - No Escape Pt 1 & 2 (Hardcastle 9)" [first cut on repeat)

[« Il avait devant lui un diamant non-taillé... ».] (dans Cahiers personnels)
["Facing him, stood an uncut-diamond..."] (in personal Notebooks)

As it had with Hemingway,
Paris had left its stigmata on his... on their soul:
A sumptuous state of mind.

The exaltation of an alternate reality:
Guided by the taboos, from all the original-sins, of *all* religions.

———

Back at his writing desk...
overlooking the early colds of a New England Fall.

The evergreen needles, apparently trying to push back the inevitability of winter-freeze.
Displaying their deepest... most *aggressive*... green!

Damn you, Hemingway!
.... and your invention of the *Movable feast*!

The crazed... demented traffic, of his first visit on rue Saint Lazard,
invading, and having replaced, the emotional emptiness
of his cherished, book-lined, shelves, around his desk.

———

The "grand café crème... tartine beurée et croissant".
The tired façade of l'église de laTrinité
with its towers, being shyly refinished under a trompe-l'oeil canvas.

This city.... like all the great, natural miracles
of an unconscious cosmos,
...
not willfully exaggerating *ITS* beauty:
...
but rather, simply presenting itself...
like HER bodily entrance into his life.

" It could not have been otherwise"...
he thought to himself.
"Facing me... stood an uncut-diamond"
... he later entered in his notebook.

He had, unknowingly, taken the emotional measure
of her every movements.
Mundane particles of a greater lyricism.
She had the youthful potential of a stem-cell.
He would compare it to...

"galaxies crashing into each other
producing new worlds... new dimensions."

———

He remembers feeling disconnected from his staid colleagues...
... even from the safety of office clutter.

She was the proverbial black hole:
whose very attraction could rewrite the genesis
of things and people.

Somehow traversing time
on waves of her feminine virility.

———

Jean-Yves Vincent Ciccariello Solinga

His dead soul,
somehow, experiencing a quasi-religious conversion.
Struck down near Saint Sulpice...
not far from Saint Germain des Prés...

... at the intersection of religious fervor and the appeal of pliable flesh.

Since those days... he had lost the youth.
But not the passion.

———

Humanity wrongly attributes to divinities
perceived intent and use of their powers.

While artists and poets, will have done all the work!

The beauty of things... time... and places...
will have been captured
on grotto-walls, blue-veined marble statues and filigreed-frescos.

———

Paris... this Paris...
is simply our very own doppelgänger
of the human imposition, of happiness,
on a dead cosmos.

And what a gorgeous beauty!!
The verbal capture of a *pregnant, knowing glance,*...
from the other side of a minuscule café table.

The swirling, hallucinating, arrogance of a Van Gogh:
capturing the ephemeral... *starlight*... in the Jeu de Paume museum.

The hypnotic glance of a Manet's nude:
forever blending sexuality and assertion
-looking down from the Orsay walls-

———

Once more... before his leaving...
the early-night.... silhouette... of a surviving Notre Dame.
He just simply... wanted to die!
Accepting his mortality.

His mortal body
displayed among all this beauty!

And like François Villon's "Balade des pendus":
this urban gallows,
would bring future indulgences from future, lover-witnesses.

He wondered...
"Did some early Parisii settler, of l'île de la Cité, look up, centuries ago...
anticipating my glance?

Death in the Barnyard

To a certain Maghreban chicken of his youth

Ah! To die like a chicken:
A last jerky movement of his beautiful crimson crest.

Nobility of his kingdom:
The unpretentious *naturel* in his demeanor.

Surrounded by his family, busily scratching... in the corner.
-out of habit-

An envious... seamless world...
of animal predictability and repetition...

Folding his legs, under his mink-white, royal plumage,
closing his third eye-lids...
HE died...
... as though for an eternal dust-bath.

Back from the oncologist.

Reincarnation

"Two Frenchmen, enter an historic, New England tavern."

In memoriam of Aymeric Dupré la Tour

A Hollywood-scripted silence welcomed them.

Old farming community of early British-settlers.
No nonsense, early-risers... for cow-milking.

And now these two effete, European-apparitions, in their midst!
However,
... seemingly, not projecting any cultural threats to their beers.

-The *retinue*, at the bar,
... benevolently scoffed at their presence.

A bottle of Remy Martin,
obligingly found, on a dusty shelf.

And then, the magic of commingling personal moments.
Times, that had brought these two men...
to these barstools.

———

It was *His* exquisite contradictions
-found only in the vast spaces of a person's soul-
that so precisely defined *him*.

A world-class refinement.
A diamond...

... that only the fertile coincidences...
of talent... knowledge and poetry... can produce.

———

And especially,
His genuinely *childlike* remarks:
On the various *geneses* of falling in love!!

-All in our mother-tongue... in this bar!-

———

I... now... fancy his last moments of consciousness...
... as deeply, breathing-in...
... Provençal, floral-perfumes, on overheated flesh.

Thus making, his own, last entrance in the down of lyricism...
... to the sound of his favorite passage, from a Liszt Lebensraum.

Ethereal crystalline notes,
from the right hand on the piano.

The ones, that would announce
-with sensual musical-phrasings-
her entrance on stage.

———

A diamond...
... that only the fertile coincidences...
of talent... knowledge and poetry... can produce.

[Note from personal journal. (from first encounter with Aymeric in Bartleby's, in downtown, Mystic Connecticut) ... " Like a reincarnation of Franz Liszt... his shoulder-length hair, very slander built and black outfit..."]

French Version of « Réincarnation »

« Deux Français, entrent dans une ancienne taverne de la Nouvelle Angleterre. »

In memoriam : Aymeric Dupré la Tour.

Un silence
digne d'un scenario de Hollywood… les accueillit.
Une vieille agglomération fermière :
des premières vagues des colons anglais.

Sérieuses personnes,
se levant tôt pour le trait des vaches.
Et maintenant,
ces deux apparitions décadentes, parmi eux !

Ne représentant, apparemment,
aucun danger culturel envers leurs bières.

———

La retenue du bar
se moqua bénévolement de leur présence.

Une bouteille de Rémy Martin
obligeamment repérée, sous la poussière d'une étagère.

Et après,
c'est la magie de mélanges des moments personnels :
Des moments,
qui amenèrent ces deux hommes…
sur ces tabourets de bar.

———

C'étaient… *SES* exquises contradictions de tempérament !
-se trouvant exclusivement dans les vastes espaces de son âme-
qui *LE* dessinaient si bien.

Une finesse
d'un niveau mondial :

Un diamant... auquel...
seules les coïncidences fertiles de talent ... de savoir et de poésie
... auraient pu donner naissance.

———

Et surtout,
Ses remarques quasiment enfantines !
Surtout celles... concernant les différentes *genèses* de l'amour !!

Et tout cela... dans notre langue maternelle... dans ce bar !

———

Quant à moi... je me représente ses derniers moments de connaissance...
... aspirant fermement les essences de parfums de Provence...
sur les chairs surchauffées.

Marquant, sa propre et dernière entrée dans le duvet du lyrisme
... au son de son passage favori d'un Lebensraum de Liszt

Notes éthérées cristallines
de la main droite du piano :
Celles, qui annonçaient
-en phrases sensuelles musicales-
l'entrée en scène de *cette femme*

———

Un diamant... auquel...
seules les coïncidences fertiles de talent ... de savoir et de poésie
auraient pu donner naissance.

[Note : dans journal personnel. (de la première rencontre avec Aymeric à Bartleby's, au centre de Mystic Connecticut) ... " Comme une réincarnation de Franz Liszt... ses cheveux à mi-dos, taille mince et habillé tout en noir"]

Duality of This Woman

Between Le Sacré Coeur and La Place Blanche

Up high, on the soil of martyrs:
Urban Virgin… Protected by white Byzantine marble.
Modern-day sufferers of all sorts of afflictions, are still crawling at your feet:
Trembling in the trove of feverish passions, of the flesh and soul.
Sanguine stigma, hidden and exposed.

Duality of *this woman*:
Urbanized Holy Virgin. Lady of stylish office suits.
Creased white blouses, with hints of black-lace support.
Un-approachable creature of city life:
In her habitat and predatory glance.

Duality of this woman:
An urban, contemporary holy-virgin, with the idealized attributes…
of the untouchable… non-approachable qualities.

All the iridescence of Temple Vestals.
Incarnation of thoughts and desires:
In this reclining presence, whose ethereal nudity, would have tested the choices of paint mounds on the palette:

Leaving the artist ambivalent:
Between his allegiance to a double nature of the subject.
Or the idealization of her flesh… still fresh with sparkles of intimacy.
The whole in…
Earthy essences… and stigmata from climatic moments.

Hommage à Jean Désiré Gustave Courbet.
Overlapping and revised images of Paris.

Monica

"I will be graduating from nursing school, this year"

Superficiality of university mixer:
She was a "red-head"!

Not unlike a James Bond movie:
Mutual glances amidst the base-beat of an English band.
Not expecting any sort of incarnation from his lyrical world:

In this meat-market of instantaneous gratification.

But appear… she did!
The "reserve and passion" of his poetic creations.
She was the galactic center
among celestial explosions and merciless shredding of young souls.

———

At first…an astonishing noble reserve…
A quasi-misplaced aristocratic demeanor:
Where he had expected a vulgar aggressivity:
He was looking into the introspective eyes of bored aloofness.

In his embrace during a slow danse:
Her sexual baggage evaporated,
with every subtle sentiment she voiced:

She was, in his soul, the very fragility of endangered species.

———

Life and Viet Nam got in the way.

She disappeared in the prosaic of everyday things
of a military nurse.

Leaving him envious for the anonymous soldiers
who would know her touch in their pain.

And maybe…. just maybe… earn her portion
of some celestial dispensation.

Inspired by "Reserve and Passion", in "Clair-Obscur of the Soul" (2008)
[Dreams and realities] (2008)

Dusty Kiss

Sometimes foreign symbols, translate seamlessly to human language.
Pulling a happy, gentle, tail-wagging puppy, out of Italian, hearth quake ruins,
after a week. [television footage]

What you would say...
to someone who had just pulled you out
of the rubbles of your collapsed bedroom?

To someone...
who was carrying you, gently in their arms:
down to the safety of the street.

To someone...
who would gingerly, wipe the sharp edges of cement:
from your *beautiful light-brown eyes!*

That someone, who would even plant, tear-laced kisses,
on your forehead...
... and yet...
not be able to verbalize your gratitude?

———

.... you would instinctively...
...*uncontrollably*...
offer visceral... body-proof of your appreciation.

And preciously wag your tail...
... for all to see!

"Corresponding, Semiotic markers between species": topic of another enlightening - Cognac-inspired- conversation, between former academics.

Armstrong's Leap

Quiet, reserved arrogance
   in this symbolic man.

Cosmological odds, greater than zero…
of an alternate Genesis of some sort of *life*.

Survival insurance and cold logic…
that any other alternate's sentient behavior
couldn't be much worse than earthlings.

Humble… but hopeful beginnings
in this desperate orphan in an empty orphanage:
that…
"They might, in turn know, the lyrical moments of life and living."

Thought poem: The astronaut Neil Armstrong, having… surreptitiously and purposefully left his feces on the Moon as seedlings for the universe.

Green-Eyed World

Like some all-purpose offerings
to the deity of the week end.

And man of the world... that he was...
Walking, confidently back in the dormitory room,
with the obligatory *two cheap beers*:

Now staring awkwardly
at a *University blind-date experience.*

Mini skirt.
Cigarette at the very tip of her index and middle finger:
As though a photo-op, imposed on her.

Like a snake ritual,
she had somehow twisted her legs.

He was mesmerized by the intertwined spectacle.

To the admiration of his floormates:
His candid reaction, softened her reputed,
impervious, mineral-soul.

(From author's notes, in "Pages of a personal mythology": surviving in a new Anglo-Saxon culture, where green-eyed girls became more commonplace.

Deconstruction of "Babar the Elephant"
A fable

Would it have been a greater loss to our world, if Africa's contribution to the earth, dominant, sentient population, had been its elephants... and not what we have become and done?

Space Odyssey...
Chimpanzees seeming to find their source of *Faustian* knowledge.
The monolith has given them their entry...
their beginnings, into some sort of self-awareness.

Their brain... our brain... our hope...
their future:
Humanity's eventual authorship of exquisite musical waves.
Such as "Blue Danube" and "thus Spoke Zarathustra".
Musical Teutonic samples of its best of "the best of worlds possible".

Finely chiseled... cultured civilizations.
Cinematographic evidence of humans,
leaving behind their hairy, bestial-smells.

And yet, to come...
the dark underside of human arrogance:
in the midst of these pearls of *conceptualized* beauty.
-In fact, blinded by THEM-

Now blooming, dormant seeds of demented, man-made horrors.
Manufactured World-Wars.

Mankind's imitation of those inflicted by mythological deities.
Such as, mindless atrocities,
on the "pro-Mankind-Prometheus"...
... for *disrespect*!

On the cosmic time and scale;
in the grayish, meaningless uniformity of galactic clouds;
what would have been inherently insulting... to us...

... had pachyderms become the predominant, intelligent entities?
Fashioning their own god...
in thick, rough skin and an impeccable green suit?

Babar... such nostalgic figure! Yet, nothing is so simple. This 'thought-poem', posits the inverse future, for the anthropomorphic animal, in a European suit. Instead, Babar and his kind, would have "inherited" the planet, instead of the hominids, who evolved from Africa to take over the globe. Where would have been the harm... except in our imaginary?

Early Fall in Saint Émilion

Early Fall in Saint Émilion
A nihilist in the vineyards of Saint Émilion

At the disheartening fracture
between the damnable nihilism in our mind
the we want to forget
and...
the hedonism in our arms
that will be leaving.

Between exists the daily dust of star dust
that fills in our eyes... the distractions of reality.

Distracting us from the grotesque ugliness of the cosmos...
because assumed.
insipid

Next velvet ephemeral purple liquid-robe against the back of the throat.

In an Open Field of New England

Immigrants leaving nonverbal traces of themselves

Immigrants having left their past behind...
Feeling a sort of primordial urge.

Not unlike prehistoric cave-dwellers, in front humid walls:
Spreading red muds, in the fluid-shape of hunters.

Did their unequal odds against time, manifest themselves,
when noticing the colors starting to run and fade?

———

These two proud men... away from all they knew.
Now, not even capable, of naming
-in the local tongue-
Things around them.

Even their flimsy shoes and clothes,
unsuited for the New England cold.

And yet...
Each... independently... in unverbalized silence...
left behind solid totems of their presence:
an enormous Maple from a skinny twig in the wet Spring dirt;
and an quasi-*immortal* stone wall:

Proper legacies, for wandering immigrants.

During a Cognac-encouraged, after dinner conversation: two sons of immigrant families, recall their grandfathers.

Half-Slumber

The insidious, economic impact of wars: "... but, young man... your status is One-A!"

Half-sleep... is made of half-truths.
It is in the escapist-domain of dreamers and poets.

He had had that recurrent dream, since March:
Leading to his waking-up in cold sweats,
in the still overheated dorm-room.

No amount of abusing alcohol would suffice.
The hang-over would go away.
Reality would not.

He instinctively reached for his wallet:
He could feel the draft letter where he had left it...

———

Her limpid blue eyes... still... sparkling with tears!
Her fingers, still nervously, twirling her blond hair.

———

The once in-the-life-time assignment:
Liaison bureau ...in Paris!

Fuzzy-skilled, humanistic opportunity!
The international-econometrics, research post still existed...
But for someone else.

Waking up in university dorm... and one day closer to bootcamp and Viet Nam.

Back to Cosmic Dust

An early-Fall walk through a cemetery.

It was just a shortcut to the post office:
An early-New England, settlers place,
for a physical link to eternity.

Serious people... with clear-eyed delineation
between the now... and the forever.

Probable former inhabitants of the near-by New England village.
Lives of cold winter nights and colder bedrooms.
Life-goals... squeezed by Biblical guideposts.

Cemetery with symbolically, Calvinistic-grey headstones,
Reflecting the austere, ethical tonality of their daily life
and disdain for opulence.

An existence of observed abnegations...
and anticipated, hopeful divine rewards.

———

But.... then... down some alleys...
A plot, showing a taste, from European visits...
for gothic side-chapels:

Some successful merchant... of mercantile trinkets...
somehow wanting "to take it with him":

Like some Latter-Day-Pharaoh
Reluctantly having become...
common, cosmic dust.

Envisioning a walk through the "cemeteries of world- history" and looking at the most diabolical names produced by mankind... with names, now covered by layers of pitted greenish moss: from another Cognac-induced comment... "... that is the difference between human and divine evil: the first one, we can solve ourselves."

El Maghreb **

"And thus, spoke youth...".

Stem-cell moments,
With unspoken understanding.

They both stopped.

Stood still... at the entrance of the cave:
Their glance upon the other.

Youth... opportunity... the heat off the rocks...
The salty coolness of the shadows.

Things were primordial:
At the stem-cell age!

Decades later...
... he still marveled at the cosmological tour de force.

Blind and dumb...
macro and minute.... energy-forces:
apparently... tenderly...
touched by the ephemeral.

*El Maghreb **[in Arabic: "The setting sun"] Visions from the cliffs of Sidi Moussa, overlooking the Atlantic Ocean, Salé, Morocco [circa 1950's]*

From the French-notebook version.

Jean-Yves Vincent Ciccariello Solinga

French Version of «El Maghreb»**

« C'est donc, ce que dit la jeunesse… »
« Thus, spoke youth… »

Moments de cellule-souche.
Communication non-verbale.
Compréhension tacite.

Ils se sont tous les deux arrêtés…
… restés immobiles … à l'entrée de la grotte :
Le regard l'un sur l'autre.

La jeunesse… l'occasion… la chaleur des roches…
La fraicheur des ombres.

Les choses étaient primordiales…
A l'âge des cellules-souche !

Des décennies plus tard…
Il s'émerveillait encore du tour de force cosmologique.

Aveugles et muettes :
ces forces énergétiques… macros et minuscules :
apparemment…et tendrement…
touchées par l'éphémère.

*El Maghreb ** [en arabe, « le soleil couchant »] regard du haut des falaises de Sidi Moussa, sur l'océan Atlantique, Salé, Maroc [circa les années 1950]*

And Humans "Constructed" the Universe

Like the rooster of the medieval fables: pretentiously thinking his crowing
wakes up the sun.

A new graduate assistant.
A miniscule room, in multi-room, urban setting:

Looking over the typically-congested "Big Dig" traffic, three stories down.

He sighed to himself:
"I should have perfected my baseball swing!"...
... when summer reflections, of the night-games,
would seem to taunt him.

———

These caustic second-thoughts of career choices:
Seemingly diluted,
in the contact of the distilled water of his table-top analyses.

———

His designated training "partner"...
No less than a world-known researcher!

———

The better fairy tales
are made of unpretentious lessons.

Gently... humanly.
...
... "If we are honest with ourselves"...
[this eminent lab-partner, whispered]
" these life-saving proteins,
have been patiently waiting to be discovered!'

Early, hopeful results of vaccine research.

Epiphany of a Nihilist

Inspired by marginal notes", for "Paris: Genesis of a Muse", of a "Personal Mythology".

Guiltless cruelty!…
He is Marlo Brando, in Paris!

Scenes of "Last Tango in Paris":
Tattooed on the soul.

Epiphany of a nihilist:
Transforming Brando into…
" L'homme de l'absurde".

His movements and actions, in this city:
where the transparency of living,
makes you aware of the silhouettes of death,
on the other side of the mirror.

The very intensity of the moment.
The immensity of sight.
The frustration of the acrid intimate smells.

The proximity of touch:
Complete, bodily synesthesia in primordial soup.

Genuine, humble human, self-awareness:
of fighting the fight,

Expanding *things*
beyond and against oblivion.

———

The Brando and Meursault personas
… as twins…
in the literary tool of nuclear fusion:

An invention...
-By humanity. For humanity-
Fiction.

Scenes of veritable visions
of an oracle of... and for hedonism.

Would reality ever match the dreams?
Feeling Henty Miller hovering overhead?

Waking-up in multiple worlds.
Poetry taking a life of its own.

In the safety of the irrational cocoon
of another half-dream sequence.

Pieces of raw carnality.
Ethereal moments *fusing* together:
Miraculously. Seamlessly.
In hedonistic sensuality.

Nuptial images...
of un-troubled innocence:
pre-dating the invention of sins.

Instead
a Hellish centrifugal attraction of primordial matter:
a combination of extreme-unction confessions.

And like a modern-day Job...
...naked in front of his god... and his word-processor...
... full of dead-silicon microchips:
Made from the dust of stars...

The language of human lyricism,
loaded into machines.

THAT... is *Humanity's glory*
over the power of a dumb universe:

ITS haunting *awareness* of time.

In Defense of Real Human Tears

He had had a natural, youthful, human impulse:
To use… verbal lyricism,
to capture the cottony-warm lubricity
emanating from the tiny bed in the tiny seventh floor
of a converted maid-room
-Rue du Bac, in Paris-

She had been introduced
to his culture in the noisy streets below:
when every sip… of Grand Café Crème
and explosions of buttery flakes from the still warm croissants

… were passports to reciprocal hedonism.

And then to so…
elegantly… so respectfully…so reservedly…
… share the "eternity of those instants"…
with a reader!

His impulse… not voyeurism
but rather to add to human introspection on happiness.

And now…
this insidious presence of coding lines…
pretending to *FEEL*…
loss… false tears… and genuine contrition.

... "Her tears were still on the pillow!"...
when she called from the airport"
... he added.

In defense of human-felt, lyricism.
Nota Bene: {AI chatbot ChatGPT [Conversational AI Platform]}... our next step toward singularity... and the increasing blurring of the recognizable "space" between silicon-chip, driven intelligence, versus the product of our "wet... squishy... gelatinous" human brain: therefore, this author's stand for authorship, made of flesh and blood, who wrote about an American student, French studies during "a steamy summer in the Paris of the 1970's"... letting his reader know that the voluptuousness of some the passages were NOT a result of some algorithms in the memory of a machine: that would have to be 'taught to cry' when she told him that she no longer loved him.

Church Festival

Memories of his first experience with a rifle [a B.B. gun] at a church festival: "He discovered an instantaneous ease and marksmanship at the "target stand", to the admiration of his father.

Like the proverbial attraction of the apple in the Garden,
His conversion had been seamless:

This instrument was his special link
to the otherwise insular paternal universe.

―――

Marginal grades in college
And time-off to "find himself"…
Left him vulnerable to being drafted.
… thus, his meteoric rise in the infantry!

Medals and ribbons later
brought him to this tearful admission
in front of a stupefied Captain:

" I can no longer look, in the cross hairs,
at a man's eyes…
… for his last ten seconds on earth…
… I can't."

A humanist sharpshooter.

Religious Sharp Shooter

Inspired by an accidental and fictionalized, conversation with a soul-searching military, ex-sharpshooter.

Bar stools...
are akin to the old fashion, church confessionals:
the anonymity is guaranteed by the loud guitar solos
and the alcohol fumes.

Each protagonist had his job description:
The confessant...
a Hollywood-sized, "good old boy" with his destroyed,
Americanized ideals.

And the confessor...
a long-time academic, European-type,
effete absurdist.

The props and scenarios for the *classical* stage:
the Biblical certainties of a sun crazed Moses
and the babblings of a Ionesco-play.

Cheap tasteless 2.5 beer...
meets Remy Martin Cognac!

The evening was pregnant with issues.
As well, as the rancid smells of overcooked fries.

———

And yet... and yet...
Humanity and humanism are resilient:

having survived worse conditions in the annals of religious atrocities,
and well-meaning cultural genocides.

Thus, the apparent cocoon of silence
that seemed to fall over the odd couple.

It flowed along with a tear-streaked whisper from the special-op officer:

"I could no longer pick up my sniper riffle...
... having seen too many human beings
... looking at me though the crosshairs
...for their last ten seconds of life!"

Les funérailles d'un père.

Retour à la rue Saint Pierre, Marseille**

Assis… dans la sombre fraîcheur d'un bistrot.
Mise en scène, apparemment parfaite…
… réalisme lyrique…
Style « Hôtel du nord ».

Abandon… silence divin et inevitable…
des hommes…
dans leur face à face aux choses.

La douleur...
… douleur sans limite… d'avoir aimé et d'avoir perdu.

Et ce regard, de l'autre côté de la table…
… de n'y reconnaitre que des réflexions vides.

Comme un gros plan de camera :
Se jouant de notre présence…

Il regarda dans les yeux, bleu-limpide de sa mère :
N'y puisant plus le bon vocabulaire.

-En aucune des deux langues-

Les langues… son baume personnel :
Sa façon de cacher les vérités et d'amoindrir la peine.

> Il avait trouvé des passages similaires dans les romans et pièces,
> qu'il avait respectueusement et professionnellement, analysés dans ses classes

Moments litteraires …d'ecrviains sages et morts :
Decrivant « la vie et l'exitence » et leur contraire :

Le silence et l'eternite

Comme un cherugien, discutant avec sang froid
Une réparation des viscères

———

Et puis… sans avertissement… avec naturel…
… servie avec gentillesse et sympathie…
cette humble tartine au Roquefort.

** (Cimetière Saint Pierre) Returning « Marseillais » to his hometown : Next to the cemetery, an empty bistro... the owner overhears the widow and her son's reason for their return to France. Without prompting, he serves them his Société Roquefort on a thickly buttered tartine !

" *Le gendarme est retourné*" [The gendarme has returned.]

A Father's Funerals

*Return to rue Saint Pierrre, Marseille***

Seated… in the cool darkness of a bistrot.
Perfect scenery… film noir style.

The lyrical realism, of « Hotel du nord »

Silent, inevitable.
Divine abandonment of mankind :

In its face to face with paiful things.
Bottomless pain :

For having loved and lost.

And this mother's glance :
from the other side of the table.

And recognizing, only empty reflections !

Like a camera close up :
Ignoring one's presence !

Looking into the limpide-blue of his mother's eyes.
No longer finding the proper vovabulaty :
In either of the two languages.

The warmth of warm words :
that used to feel like a personal balm.

His way of hidding truths and lessening the pains.

Using similar anguish passages in novels and plays :
Dutifully. Professionaly.
All respecftully analysed,
Literary moments
-from wise and dead writers -
Describing « life and living » and their antithesis :
Silence and eternity.

Like a surgeon …coolly …discussing
the intricacies of rearanging a patient's viscera !

A father's and husband's life and image in the balance.

And then ! Without warning !
Gesture full of Pathos
from the patron !
A « tartine au Roquefort »
is served…
… They had overheard about our craving for good French chesses !!

* (Cimetière Saint Pierre) A returning « Marseillais » to his hometown : Next to the cemetery, an empty bistro… the owner overhears the widow and her son's reason for their return to France : the funeral of the Gendarme ! Without prompting, the chef serves them, his Société Roquefort, on a thickly buttered tartine!

" *Le gendarme est retourné*" *[The gendarme has returned …he whispers tearfully.]*

The Temerity of Innocence

Marseille, "le Panier"*** circa 1920

Young mother, dead of "Spanish" flu...
Impoverished Neapolitan immigrants.

Ne'er-do-well father:
Having discharged his last bag of coffee, in skin-ripping hemp.

Quasi-biblical assembly of aunts, dressed in mourning-black.
And...
... traditional, freshly bathed and groomed,
remains of the mother: displayed on immaculate sheets.

And... this swirling presence of joy:
Newly orphaned little girl,
In her favorite Sunday outfit.

Comment from "tante Rose":
With a physique constructed like a centenary olive tree.
Witness of the Crimean war and two more to come.

Whispering with beatitude toward the contradictory scene:
"Don't worry... She'll survive!"

Poem, inspired by reports of storks, in Ukraine, (re)building their nests within sight and within hours of local fighting at Kharkiv bridge.

le Panier*** The "shopping basket" is an old neighorhood in Marselle.

Jean-Yves Vincent Ciccariello Solinga

For a Post-Paradisiac, Digital World

"The continuous need for passwords reminds us of our innate intelligence, as well as our classical flaws." (another attempt to fix humanity, with a "last Cognac" for the night.)

Like quaint museum representations:
Blissfully uncomplicated.

The innocent nudity of Adam and Eve:

Dark, greenish temptations of evil,
in the luxuriant background.

So easily obvious,
under its repulsive, reptilian skin!

Instead of its insidious, organic... familial genesis:
Born of a very human need to know.

Sentient intelligence: without directions for usage.
Dangers... not so easily identifiable.

We invent.
We cannot help ourselves.

Humanity... miraculously talented.
Fatally incorrigible.

The enemy being internal:
We'll have to conjure more passwords.

Reflections on entering endless passwords for new accounts: wondering about both the innovations and fatal flaws of human nature: i.e. for example, creating the conveniences of the internet: its software and hardware... and almost instantaneously, giving rise to the first "spam" and hacking. .

Lo Spasimo Della Vergine

To Yevhenii: the son of the crying mother from the village of Buzova, Ukraine.

This poem has, as its background, "The Swoon of the Virgin", in Italian [Lo Spasimo Della Vergine, or Fainting Virgin Mary]: an idea developed in the late Middle Ages, that the Virgin Mary had fainted during the Passion of Christ (most often placed while she watched the Crucifixion of her son).

A mother's inconsolable pain,
captured in respectable skin-smooth marbles:

The body of her dead son,
forming an elegant arch over her knees.

In this...the alternate reality of recreated realities,
that live in the universe of museums.

Revered scenes of revered moments:
Monumentally-established casts of characters:

In the quiet corners
of our clean and educated conscience.

———

And yet again...
the alternate universe of the arts ...keeps invading one's reality.

This one, carried by waves of her visceral wailing
... literally made...
of this man's flesh and blood.

No avatar... or go-between.

No artful Spasimo.
Just repeated... earthy... wet tears.

Of Proustian Madeleines and Camembert

Reflections on Hemingway's "A movable feast" and the pivotal role that Paris had played on a returning Viet Nam War, draft-refugee, in his twenties.

She had given him refuge... hearing now...
about the war...
... from the safety of her arms.

Only distant echoes, from the evening news.

———

Keeping him "captive" with what he would call...
" an illegal... unconventional, act of war":

His favorite camembert!

Her crémier
apparently... on her demand:
stocking an inexhaustible supply!

———

Many years later...
like recurring Proustian Madeleines...

... he could effortlessly, still reconstruct
her knowing smile...

... before setting the table .

Wisps of Her

Still here... next to me... after all this time!

Like a Courbet... hidden in one's attic:
A priceless, emotional acquisition,
made at the *contingency* of Boulevard Saint Germain
and an over-the-shoulder glance.

The universe had stopped.

There was a rich mixture of sanguine carnality in the air...
of the conviction of life beyond mortality.
The very sensuality of oil paints,
controlling the febrility of the brushstrokes.

———

He had discussed these visuals, as an academic:
Trying to coolly decipher these visions for his students...
while tortured, by his own damning ones.

And then... finding *Her* again: under the dust and spider-webs
-at the eleven O'clock-hour-
looking for scribbled recollections of this Parisian trip.

Unfurling streams of waves, upon lyrical waves of words:
Her Genesis,
whose presence in his world,
had been formed, in warm, organic secretions.

Gently preserving, in its mucus,
the barely audible, uncontrolled sighs in both languages...
somehow transcending mundane realities.

Jean-Yves Solinga in Paris

Jean-Yves Solinga, Poet

The literary landscape of Jean-Yves has vacillated between North Africa, Provence, and New England since his earliest teenage poems, written in the contradictory emotional, hedonistic setting of a post-dance embrace on frozen snow… and memories of the "little beach" off the North African continent and his surrounding "New Englandish" reality. His poetry, furthermore, jumps seamlessly between the cultural archetypes of the various influences of his life: the Arabic Sidi Moussa, the Provençal Notre Dame de la Garde of Marseille, and the teenage gods of his new World… such as "Rebel Without a Cause". So Bi-polar would therefore be an appropriate descriptive for this poetic world. It is a world torn between languages and cultures. It craves absolutes with the conviction of an atheist; and a Faustian fever, thirsty for youth, with an impending clear-eyed philosophical analysis of impending decrepitude on the horizon.

Jean-Yves' poetry exists through the various landscape of many of these poems: "guided" by Sidi Moussa the Arabic Moses of the Bible: the patron saint of the wanderer.

The coldness of the Labrador current haunts the reader with images of Sidi Moussa in the warm setting that surrounded the youth of the narration. It is, more specifically, the name of a miniscule beach north of Salé in Morocco.

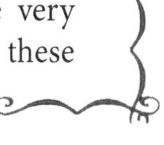

The themes sneak their way through two worlds: one, of the thematic universality of Classicism, and the other, that of the very personal individualistic emphasis of Romanticism. It is when these worlds are in complementary equilibrium - one person versus society, the first person singular versus plural, the lonely artist at his desk versus his audience in a full theatre - that the words, the painting, the artistic expression break out of the solidity of the present and make the future reader or viewer still hold his breath. Because, the best art is the one that has the feel of authenticity. Of personal immediacy of the writer, as well as the capacity to allow the viewer to take possession of a piece of it. The way that one walks with glazed eyes through museums and looks nonchalantly at a painting; returns and then stops breathlessly as though he had painted the scene himself in another life. Or the unease caused by a scenario of a movie that seems to put a piece of our life on the screen: that line where classicism, in its eternal applications, meets romanticism, in its intimate and personal projection on the viewer. Even when the expression is circumstantial and personal, it is especially in the way the reader eventually sees herself or himself in the text that can give relevance and ultimately value to the poem. One, for instance, does not have to know personally the dissolute life of the Paris of Baudelaire to understand the void of his soul. And so it is that, like Baudelaire or Camus, Jean-Yves uses religious artifacts and references to build antithetical contrasts with the fleshy amoral present. His poetry continues his wanderings between another two poles, two concepts: The fragile, ephemeral weight of a human thought and the enormity of the stuff of the universe. And the human intellect finds pieces of itself in the universe and yet, still feels alone. This is not new; but became Jean-Yves's calling, on that winter's night, driving back, from graduate studies at the University, at Storrs, when that little beach (Sidi Moussa), spoke with its hot breath on the nape of his neck. A sort of dialog, with the "desert-shepherd"—the Mose—and the narrator/writer, of his poetry. Thus, his writing began to take form. It became the driving/guiding energy, for the genesis of his work.

The North-African landscape of his youth would indirectly allow, for both, research-study, as well as, rich lyricism: As exemplified and described in the segment of the very first paragraph of Noces (epigraph) by Albert Camus. For, Jean-Yves was struck by Camus' easy combination of crystalline, succinct thought, and yet, the fine lace of his poetic sentences: Seamlessly blended into the historic, cultural, and humanistic. Simply. Describing moments. Glances!... His thoughts are inhabited by biblical figures, even if in a nihilistic, non-traditionally religious world.

Jean-Yves wrote that humans seem to have been "endowed" with the improbable luck of having evolved the ability, to reflect on their own reflections: adapting, and often using, the tool of lyricism, to reflect on these moments. Using, for instance, the artistic drive, powered by creativity, as a practical antidote to the absurdity of life: Lyricism has a way of making the absurd... calculable. So that, for instance, one should see an intellectually, "happy" Monet... dying, while looking at one of his garden scenes.

Some of the poems in his books, take note of one of humanity's real pride: Its arrogance (even if, doomed) of superiority over the dumb/blind cosmos: prompted by an amazing, university-level YouTube program, about cutting-edge topics of cosmology and physics: concluding by this remark: "Isn't it just "so human," but to impose our control over the universe, by simply writing equations about it? Poets do the same by writing poetry.

Nothing is more controlling than using the measure of the speed of light, encapsulating it in an equation, in an attempt to enlighten us! As though, the speed gives it gravitas. To then, be told that it does curve and takes corners around big masses... it is particles... it is waves... it goes untold distances apparently through nothing. Or... maybe now that the universe might (after all) be filled with "stuff" [black matter]. Got it?

All the while, our unassuming artist, seems to have been better equipped to fully join the camps of poetry AND solidity. The two poles, previously mentioned. This is on display in one of Jean-Yves's poems where the narrator, is confronted on such convoluted and expansive things as "a lecture on the beginning of time," or some similar issue... and the reader's focus is turned to the microcosm of a co-ed sitting a few feet from Jean-Yves!

Or a lyrical daydream, with post-carnal visions, worthy of a Caravaggio canvas, that turns the reader's attention to earthy happiness. And yet, the narrator/protagonist, still mentions this vaporous glance.

After all, isn't this sensual presence next, to him, on the lumpy bed in Paris, not as much a reality of the cosmos?

Since Jean-Yves first readings of Albert Camus and that first page of Noces à Tipasa, he had, specifically, found the comfortable, human, organic-rich, dirt as a metaphor for the eternal, yet fragile human happiness: Anchored in the eternal solidity of the stardust-substance... that is, the Mediterranean shoreline.

Even with the inevitable decrepitude predicted by time, and his difficult return to see and smell "le Vieux Port de Marseille" of his parents, he nevertheless wants nothing to do with the frigidity of some philosophies that, sometimes speak, in bitter terms, of human truths found in the bitter human condition. Or yet, its opposite: The bromide of escapism.

Jean-Yves prefers the likes of a Docteur Rieux, Sisyphus and Prometheus: simple men, titans, fighting the gods and their laws!

He likes to sprinkle living on the dirt of realism, as best as possible. Not unlike Camus, proposing to his reader, to consider Sisyphus happy, as he rolls his boulder under the generous sun.

Or, for instance, recalling his parents' tales of Oncle Jules, who, at the height of misery, of an occupied France, and during the added tactical mistake of an errant American bombing-raid over French civilians, ran back to the house, down the street, in order to retrieve the straw-wrapped wine bottle. He made it back safely; but Jean-Yves put this touching human trait on the same level as our unknown ancestor who went to the back of his cave to spread colored mud [probably feces-incrusted] to glorify, to this day, the wild game that gave food.

Although at ease in his nihilistic corner of the universe, He, like other writers, used the wealth of religions and various beliefs, codes, commandments, and restrictions to his advantage. Some of the best literature has evolved from violations of the norms.

Jean-Yves contemplates a rebellious prophet Abraham, who without hesitation, challenges the divine command to kill his own son: putting his son's welfare above the wishes of his God. Hence, he could have changed the genesis of a whole trace of Western, human, and religious thought. It is, indeed, much harder, dangerous, and weightier, to be rebellious like Sisyphus or Prometheus.

He writes applied fiction: Therefore, not unlike the way we prepare a student with the precepts of analyzing and looking at the world with arithmetic or advanced mathematics, but without going over every possibility. You give the student a ruler and tell him: "Now, go measure something!"

There is a difficult topic that required an adjustment in the fictionalization of reality: his French identity in the Maghreban world: answered in a non-verbal and symbolic way, with the precious picture of Jean-Yves with Barka in her djellaba. No need to write a geo-political treatise... a little boy's tearful wave settled that argument years ago.

Jean-Yves feels that experience of living, and the observation of human behavior, give the artist enough material to extrapolate. The addition of flexibility of language, the shades of paint, etc.... are a matter of choice and particular talent and interest of the artist. A budding writer of great tales, in High School today, is going to use the same words as those used by Shakespeare but for his own purpose. In theory, all the necessary material is available.

Non-fiction [i.e., "real" reality] writing demands scrupulous research. Although, history-based melodramas, allow for reconstructive fillers. (with some raising of eyebrows: "Did the Queen really say that to her husband?")

Like Proust, Jean-Yves likes the flexible safety of the "pastiche": Where the artist can combine personalities or modify them at will. So that, even in a poem based on war-time, recalled or retold to me, the writer can always change major details or leap-frog between events.

And finally, Jean-Yves wrote: We have constructed gods: We surely can construct realities. And nothing more valuable to a writer's ears than: "She [it] sounds so real: Who is she? [of a fictional feminine presence]

Other Books by Jean-Yves Solinga

Clair-obscur de l'âme

Clair-Obscur of the Soul

In the Shade of a Flower

Landscape of Envies

Words Made of Silk

Impressions of Reality

Artist in a Pixelated World

Asymptotes at the Infinity of Passion

Created Reality

Paris: Genesis of a Muse

Rage and Passion